The adult development of C. G. Jung

John-Raphael Staude

The adult development of C. G. Jung

Routledge & Kegan Paul
Boston, London and Henley

First published in 1981
by Routledge & Kegan Paul Ltd
9 Park Street,
Boston, Mass. 021908, USA,
39 Store Street,
London WC1E 7DD and
Broadway House,
Newtown Road,
Henley-on-Thames,
Oxon RG9 1EN

Set in 11/12 Journal Roman
by Academic Typesetting, Gerrards Cross, Bucks
and printed in the United States of America

British Library Cataloguing in Publication Data

Staude, John-Raphael
The adult development of C. G. Jung.
1. Adulthood
2. Developmental psychology
I. Title
155.6   BF724.5

ISBN 0-7100-0749-3

Contents

For my teachers:

Carl E. Schorske, historian
Robert N. Bellah, sociologist
Nevitt A. Sanford, psychologist
James Hillman, Jungian analyst

Preface

The field of adult development is a relatively new one. While there has been a considerable elaboration of theory and empirical research about child development and adolescence in the study of human development, until recently there has been a tendency among psychologists and social scientists to assume that development ends with the achievement of biological maturity in early adulthood. The very word 'adulthood' has none of the concreteness that we feel for such terms as 'childhood' or 'adolescence.' Very often 'adulthood' is used very loosely as a catchall category for everything that happens to the individual human being after reaching biological maturity or after a specific chronological age, such as twenty-one. Recently, life-span developmental psychologists have begun to chart and analyze the stages of development in later life and to consider the aging process in the context of life-cycle theory (Baltes and Schaie, 1973). Despite this growing interest in the entire human life cycle, we still know far too little about the stages and developmental tasks of adult life.[1] We know something about adolescence, the transition from childhood to adulthood, but we know much less about the mid-life transition, and even less about the post-climacteric late-life transition. All in all, adulthood in contemporary society is still generally viewed in much too undifferentiated a manner. We still lack a comprehensive theory of adult development.

Given that the field of adult development is so new and undeveloped, it is not surprising that at present there is no generally accepted theory or even empirically tested concepts currently available. We need many more empirical studies before such a theory can emerge. I have, therefore, chosen to focus my book on a study of adult development and the aging process in the life of Carl Gustav Jung, a distinguished pioneer in adult developmental psychology.

In my work I show how Jung developed his interpretation of what he called 'the individuation process' during the second half of life out of his own personal and clinical experience. I have concentrated on his mid-life crisis, following his own view that these were the most important years in his life, the time in which 'everything essential was decided' (Jung, 1961). This experience provided him with the prime material for his lifework:

> It has taken me virtually forty-five years to distill within the vessel of my scientific work the things I experienced and wrote down at that time. As a young man my goal had been to accomplish something in my science. But then I hit upon this stream of lava, and the heat of its fires reshaped my life. That was the primal stuff which compelled me to work upon it, and my works are a more or less successful endeavor to incorporate this incandescent matter into the contemporary picture of the world (Jung, 1961, p. 199).

Jung's work is really only comprehensible when viewed from the perspective of his own personal and intellectual development, particularly in his middle and late adulthood.

My method is phenomenological. I have attempted to view Jung's development from inside, as felt and experienced, as well as to view it in the social historical context in which he lived. My overall framework is that of life-span developmental psychology, but my emphasis is on the major turning points and transitions in Jung's life and his response to them. In this way I have attempted to link the development of his theory with his own developmental processes.

This study is organized in the following manner. In the first chapter I survey the history of life-span developmental psychology and discuss the emergence of 'adult development' as a subspecialty within the discipline. I then place Jung in the context of other pioneers in the field such as G. Stanley Hall, Charlotte Bühler and Erik Erikson. Finally, I briefly indicate the state of the field today, as I see it. In the second chapter I discuss Jung's personal and intellectual development as a scholar-physician during the years 1900 to 1912. During these years Jung formed a preliminary adult identity. He made some major choices regarding his occupation, marriage, residence and style of living that defined his place in the adult world. He developed a relationship with a mentor, and eventually broke with his mentor, Freud, in order to develop his own ideas. In my third chapter I emphasize the developmental tasks Jung faced at mid-life and the way in which he worked through them, dissolving his old life structure and developing a new one in the period 1912 to 1922. In my fourth chapter I show that Jung developed his theory of the individuation process in the second half of life out of his own personal experience. I focus particularly on his writings in 1916 immediately after he emerged from his mid-life breakdown. I show how he developed the technique of 'active imagination' as a way of working with images and how he articulated his new hard-won insights in his book *Psychological Types.* Finally, I discuss his developmental theory and relate it to the changes he experienced as he moved into the second half of his life.

In my conclusion I evaluate Jung's contributions to adult developmental psychology and consider the limitations of his theory which was so tied to his own personality type. I argue that Jung's archetypal psychology complements and supplements the ego-psychology of mainstream developmental theory. The implications of Jung's psychology for life-span developmental psychology are profound. Instead of focusing on the achievement of ego competencies, Jung evaluated lives in terms of their balance, well-roundedness, wholeness. He emphasized developing the underdeveloped aspects of the self and maintaining an ongoing dialogue between the ego and non-ego aspects of the self as a total self-regulating developing system. Jung's theory offers a compensatory view to the ego-psychology dominating life-span developmental psychology today.

Before I became a psychologist and a sociologist, I was a European intellectual historian. My first book (1968) was an intellectual biography of Max Scheler (1874–1928), a multi-dimensional personality – philosopher, sociologist, and culture critic who was known as 'the Catholic Nietzsche' for his ascerbic critique of modern culture and society. At that time I developed an admiration for Scheler and for the broad multidisciplinary approach that he and other German scholars of his generation, like Carl Jung, Martin Buber, and Albert Einstein, embodied.

What first attracted me to writing a book about Jung was the publication of his letters, especially the correspondence with Freud. As a biographer and intellectual historian, living in Zurich at that time, how could I resist such an opportunity? Through my contact with Scheler's life and work, I had become a sociologist. I had no intention of becoming a Jungian analyst upon enrolling at the Jung Institute to participant observe Jungian psychology at the source. My way of working has always been to expose myself as directly as possible to my sources. In the 1960s when writing on youth and religion I lived in caves and communes with my informants. So I found myself in Swiss-German Zurich, the land of 'No, Thou shalt not. . . .' As an extroverted Roman Catholic of Mexican-Italian, French and Jewish descent, I found the withdrawn stolid Swiss-German Protestant lifestyle difficult to live with. I soon realized that Jungian analysis is not only a kind of socialization for introversion, but corresponds to the ruminating inner-directed temperament of alpine peoples. After a suitable period of initiation, I moved across the alps to live in one of Jung's favorite spots, the Eranos Foundation in Ascona on lovely Lago Maggiore.

The library at Eranos was excellent, as was the Swiss-Italian food and culture, which softened the impact of my weekly analytic and training sessions in Zurich with James Hillman and other members of the Institute.

Members of the Jung family and the Jungfrauen viewed my project with some suspicion. They were helpful, but Franz Jung wondered how I could ever understand his father's life and thought since I was not a Swiss psychiatrist myself. As an historian, he suggested I might better spend my time studying Bismarck. At the Institute my sociologically oriented questions were often parried with the rejoinder that something must be amiss in my psyche and I should consult my dreams and my analyst about my 'sociological fantasies.'

I must admit that the sanctimonious and reverential attitude towards Jung one finds around the Institute, particularly among the clergy and ex-Protestant ministers who made up the majority of the student body while I was there, brought out the irreverent imp in me. I enjoyed tantalizing them with diabolical and provocative questions as I had enjoyed upsetting my Jesuit teachers earlier in my life. Jungians would say that the goody-goody quality of the devoted students constellated my 'shadow side.'

In any case, the lectures of Professors Hillman, David Miller, and Giles Quispel and Marie-Louise von Franz were a welcome relief from the rather catechetical atmosphere of most of the other classes I attended. In the end, I did not take a diploma from the Institute, but returned to the United States to complete my psychological training there and in London.

Instead of writing the intellectual biography of Jung I had originally set out to do, like Hans Castorp, after seven years, I fled from the magic mountains of Switzerland and returned to the flatlands of university research, armed with my knowledge of Jungian psychology, but determined to ground myself once again in history, sociology, and academic psychology, a less solipsistic, if less imaginative and fanciful tradition. The present book is the result of my effort to come home from the magic mountain.

In this book I combine a knowledge of theory and methods of lifespan developmental psychology with training in comparative sociology and European social and cultural history. To understand the development of personality and generativity through the entire life course, a biographical, historical, sociological, and psychological approach is necessary. Psychology is not enough. We must think about the nature of society and the individual's participation in it via social roles and careers, family life, social class and social movements, generations and generational change. In short we must study individual lives in social and historical contexts. 'The biographical study of lives enables us to study the personality in greater depth, complexity and relevance for both individual and society' (Levinson, 1980).

The framework for analyzing the data of this study is a historically informed lifespan psychology appropriate to the complex multidimensionality of the creative personality. Too often studies of the developmental flow of lives of individuals give the false impression that individuals develop in a socio-historical vacuum. While psychology has had much to say about the individual's relationships with other individuals, it has usually ignored the individual's relationships with groups, institutions and other social systems. The study of these relationships has been left largely to history, sociology and anthropology. In the usual sociological study, on the other hand, too often the individual life is seen as a set of social roles governed almost entirely by social structure. Less attention has been given to the psychological aspects of the person's relationship with the social group, or to the ways in which the individual personality enters into the formation, enactment and evolution of social roles. It is equally important to avoid a psychological reductionism which regards the individual's social participation as merely derivitive of inner fantasies, motives, cognition functions or habits. Such reductionism 'makes society an epiphenomenon, an outgrowth of individual psychology, but not a major influence on the individual life course' (Levinson, 1980). What is needed, and what I do in this study, is to bring together psychological, sociological, and historical perspectives. This work combines rigorous social, historical, and biographical analysis based on primary and secondary documents with analytical models drawn from psychoanalytic theory and lifespan developmental psychology.

In the tradition of Drs Else Frenkel-Brunswik and Charlotte Buhler, carried on by Henry Murray, Robert White, and Daniel Levinson, I believe we must begin from 'biographical psychology,' the study of individual lives in context in order to build our theory of adult personality development. I agree with Bernice Neugarten (1964) that:

> A developmental theory of adult personality is likely to emerge only after . . . more of the relevant dimensions have become measurable. In the meantime the investigator will proceed patiently with the descriptive studies that must be carried out first, in the confidence that both his theories and his more rigorous research designs must grow from, rather than precede, systematic observations on normal adults.

Every theory of development is a construct drawn from the richness of lived experience. Lives are always more complex and interesting than any model or theoretical construct that can be imposed on them. Therefore, in this study I have sought to maintain a balance between the nomothetic style of some psychological and sociological analyses and the ideographic style of some humanities and historical scholarship. This work combines rigorous social historical analysis based on empirical research on primary and secondary documents with the research instruments and models developed in lifespan psychology. Whereas the humanist aims at 'the greatest possible illumination of a cultural product, relativizing all principles of analysis to its particular content,' I seek to locate and interpret the artifact temporally in a field where two lines intersect. With the diachronic or vertical line I establish the relation of the text to Jung's life course and to the history of psychology or previous expressions of the same kind of cultural activity. With the other synchronic or horizontal line I assess the relation of Jung's life and work to other lives and to what was appearing in other areas of the social and cultural system at the same time (Schorske, 1980, p. xxii).

As a historian, I want to offer a few reflections on Jung's place in modern intellectual history and social theory. Intellectually, Jung belonged to the anti-historicist generation born in the late nineteenth century for whom Nietzsche was the mentor of their youth. In contrast to Marx, Durkheim, Pareto, Weber, and Freud, the founding fathers of the social sciences, for whom History and Society were realities *sui generis*, for Jung's generation the nineteenth-century belief in progress had evaporated. 'History seemed no longer to contain the cosmic secret, as the nineteenth century had believed' (Luft, 1980). Jung's generational contemporaries included men born in the 1870s such as Karl Kraus, Hugo von Hofmannsthal, and Max Scheler (1874), Emil Lask, Thomas Mann, and Rainer Maria Rilke (1875), Hermann Hesse (1877), and Martin Buber and Alfred Doblin (1878). Among those born in the 1880s were Robert Musil, Oswald Spengler, and Otto Weininger (1880), Karl Jaspers and Franz Kafka (1883), Ernst Bloch, Erich Kahler, and Georg Lukács (1885), Karl Barth, Gottfried Benn, Hermann Broch, and Paul Tillich (1886). Martin Heidegger and Ludwig Wittgenstein were born in 1889.

> Setting out from the uncertainty of knowledge and the inadequacy of every form of dogmatism the thinkers of this generation were conscious of the fragility and brevity of human civilization. Although they often moved to broader sociological and ideological analysis after World War I, their fundamental impulse was psychological, ethical, and aesthetic, focused on the inner crisis of their culture. Confronted with the decline of the old cosmologies of progress, they sought to reawaken the positive value of the unconscious, sexuality, and dream life. This meant the new importance of symbolism, of language as a medium

(or prison) unto itself, and of the unconscious as a source of creativity. Although they sought to overcome the pessimism of the 1890s, theirs was an optimism over the abyss, at the edge of suicide and despair, a vitalism in the face of a preoccupation with biological reductionism and death. It was in part their sense of loss of a coherent ideology which eventually facilitated the rise of fascism. (Luft, 1980, p. 17)

In his memoirs Jung tells us that he grew up in Basel in the shadow of the Middle Ages. His critique of modernity, like that of Scheler, Lagarde, Langbehn and other conservative religious critics of massification, mass man, and mass society, grew in part out of his inability and unwillingness to adapt to the changing world around him (Giner, 1976). He looked back from the security of the magic mountains of peaceful German Protestant Switzerland to the cosmopolitan pre-nationalist pre-industrial Europe of the eighteenth century, and beyond that to the Middle Ages and antiquity. Totally put off by the upheaval of the World War and the Russian Revolution, Jung could only warn Europeans to return to their Protestant Christian heritage of self-reflection. Like Scheler, Jung urged modern man to repent his arrogance and materialism, to return to his religious roots, and recover his lost soul (Staude, 1968):

Every individual needs revolution, inner division, overthrow of the existing order, and renewal, but not by forcing them upon his neighbors under the hypocritical cloak of Christian love or the sense of social responsibility or any of the other beautiful euphemisms for unconscious urges to personal power. Individual self-reflection, return of the individual to the ground of human nature, to his own deepest being with its individual and social destiny – here is the beginning of a cure for that blindness which reigns at the present hour. Interest in the problem of the human psyche is a symptom of this instictive return to oneself. (Jung, 1966a, p. 5)

Like other members of his generation, Jung rejected the ethos of modern technology and bureaucracy. This ethos is characterized by mechanicalness, reproducibility, and measurability, producing abstraction, functional rationality, instrumentality in human relationships and alienation in the soul of modern man. In Jung's view, modern man had become overcivilized, cut off from his roots in nature and the psyche. The 'death of God,' the demise of traditional religion, and the failure of bourgeois social and cultural traditions to capture their allegiance evoked ideological creativity from Jung and his generation. With historical hindsight we can now see that they had more in common with their nineteenth-century ancestors than with the nihilistic children of 1914. The 'quest for meaning' which Jung discovered to be the task of the 'second half of life,' in fact was also the quest of his generation grappling with the uncertainties of the twentieth century.

> I am neither spurred on by excessive optimism nor in love with high ideals, but am merely concerned with the fate of the individual human being – that infinitesimal unit on whom a world depends, and in whom, if we read the meaning of the Christian message aright, even God seeks his goal. . . . Does the individual know that he is the makeweight that tips the scales? (Jung, 1970b)

Jung warned of our general 'moral backwardness' which has not kept pace with our technological and social progress. Speaking out like his prophetic grandfather, the Dean of the Cathedral of Basel, Jung denounced the normlessness and short-sighted opportunism of modern man. He warned that modern man had sold out his birthright, his life-preserving myth preserved in Protestant Christianity and tradition for the fool's gold of modernity and secularization.

In a fundamental way, Jung was anti-historical and anti-political in the same sense that Plato, Schopenhauer, and Nietzsche were anti-historical and anti-political. Behind the panorama of historical events and the melodrama of personal history, Jung looked for the eternal play and transformation of archetypal images, patterns and structures. Protestations to the contrary, most Jungians have a very undeveloped historical consciousness. Like their mentor and master, they tend to be more interested in the eternal archetypal forms than in the flux of historical and social change.

For example, Jung's work on alchemy offers many perceptive insights to the cultural historian, but must be read with caution for in Jung's mind past and present were almost interchangeable. He saw no problem in using the dreams of a twentieth-century patient to interpret obscure passages in the writings of sixteenth- and seventeenth-century alchemists. What is lacking in Jung's essays in historical hermeneutics is an adequate grasp of the interplay between culture and social structure, that mesocosm – to use Joseph Campbell's concept – that mediates archetypal structures in historical life (Note see my essay on Freud, Jung and Lévi-Strauss in *Theory and Society*, 3 (1976) and Ira Progoff's fine book *Jung's Psychology and its Social Meaning*.)

James Hillman (1972, 1975a, 1975b, 1979) and James Olney (1972, 1980) rightly place Jung in the Platonic and neo-platonic Augustinian intellectual tradition. For a time I sought to write a book that would articulate Jung's connection with the Platonic and Hermetic traditions, but abandoned the effort and ruefully dragged myself to shore having almost drowned in the writings of medieval mystics and gnostics, if not in Jung's murky collected works. Olney eventually abandoned a similar project, and concentrated instead on exploring the relationship between Jungian thought and the pre-Socratic philosophers as well as Plato. He rationalized his retreat by concluding that

> to treat of such figures in the tradition as Hermes Trismegistus, Philo Judaeus, the Gnostics, the various Neoplatonists, St. Augustine, Pseudo-Dionysius, Paracelsus, Boehme, Swedenborg, the Cambridge Platonists, and Blake would merely obscure the clarity of the lines so painstakingly sought out by a return to antiquity. (Olney, 1980, p. 23n)

While it is certainly true that Jungian thought grows out of what he called 'the rhizome' of the Platonic tradition, the same may be said of a major part of Western European intellectual and cultural history and tradition. In the long run, as Whitehead said, we are all either Platonists or Aristotelians; Jung made a similar observation in *Psychological Types*. Thus, to show how Jung was a Platonist at heart does not tell us enough to anchor him historically and intellectually. In my opinion, the key to Jung's social and intellectual foundations lies in the German Protestant, bourgeois, romantic idealist tradition of the late eighteenth and early nineteenth century. In the fantasy life of his youth, Jung had imagined himself to be a well groomed gentleman of the eighteenth century, when in fact he was but a poor little schoolboy, the humble son of the local parson in a tiny village. As an eighteenth-century gentleman he had power, wisdom and style and could imagine himself commanding the respect which he did not receive as the poor parson's son. This idealization of himself as an eighteenth-century German also linked him personally to the creators of classical German literature and thought – Goethe, Schiller, Holderlin, Novalis, and the philosophers Kant, Leibniz, Schopenhauer, Schelling, Fichte, and Hegel. His intellectual roots lay in German classicism, romanticism and idealism, a world of order and stability which contrasted greatly to the rapidly modernizing world around him from which he felt so alienated.

Interestingly, at the end of his life, in an interview on his eightieth birthday, Jung observed delightedly that he had recently discovered his precursor. The man who had articulated many ideas and experiences similar to Jung's was a great man who lived in the eighteenth century. With a mischievous twinkle in his eye he dared his interlocutor to guess who this great man might be. Kant, Goethe, Hegel? No. The Hasidic Rabbi Baer from Meseritz, the Great Maggid, said Jung, wearing the rabbinical cap he had taken to wearing since his cabalistic visions when he lay for weeks in a coma on the threshold of death in 1944. In this old eighteenth-century rabbi, as in the Gnostics and Alchemists, Jung found a kindred spirit, one of his spiritual ancestors.

Although he idealized the eighteenth century, Jung was thoroughly a nineteenth-century man. The models and heroes of his youth were the Basel neo-humanists Jakob Burckhardt, Johann Jakob Bachofen, and Friedrich Nietzsche, who had taught at the Basel Gymnasium as well as at the university, shortly before Jung's time there. In his memoirs, Jung recalled how impressed he was as a boy when he passed the great historians Burckhardt and Bachofen conversing at Bachofen's doorstep on the cathedral square. The neo-humanist ideals of classical culture and the Renaissance man were as influential on young Jung as the Protestant Christianity of his father, grandfather, his mother, and his uncles, most of whom were Protestant ministers. Burckhardt and Nietzsche were also pastor's sons and Bachofen, scion of a family of wealthy merchants, stood in the same Protestant tradition which required a sense of duty, frugality, civic consciousness, and propriety.

Reading the neo-humanists' interpretations of classical antiquity, made all the more vivid by the classical frescoes painted by Arnold Böcklin for the Basel City Hall and Museum in the 1880s, Jung felt drawn to study classical archeology when he went to university. It was financial considerations, as well as a love of science, that led him to opt for medicine instead. Like other scholars of his generation he had been required to study the classics in the original languages at school. His father, who had taken his doctorate in ancient classical and biblical studies, coached him at home. By the time he reached high school, he was so good at Latin that his teacher encouraged him to do advanced independent studies. Even in his old age Jung read Latin easily for pleasure.

Perhaps as a result of his nineteenth-century classical education, Greco-roman mythology and history were so important and 'real' for Jung – more real in fact than the puzzling world of the twentieth century. In fact, Jung was so imbued with the classical spirit that he turned to ancient myth as a reference point throughout his life. What Thomas Mann said in his old age about the meaning of myth to ancient man applies to some extent also to Jung. In his beautiful essay on Freud, Mann wrote:

The word *Tiefenpsychologie* [depth psychology] has a
temporal significance; the primitive foundations of the
human soul are likewise primitive time, they are those
profound time sources where the myth has its home and
shapes the primeval norms and forms of life. For the
myth is the foundation of life; it is the timeless schema,
the pious formula into which life flows when it repro-
duces its traits out of the unconscious. . . . While in the
life of the human race the mythical is an early and primitive stage, in the life of the individual it is a late and
mature one. What is gained is an insight into the higher
truth depicted in the actual, a smiling knowledge of the
eternal. . . .

The ego of antiquity and its consciousness of itself
were different from our own, less exclusive, less sharply
defined. It was, as it were, open behind; it received much
from the past and by repeating it gave it presentness
again. The Spanish scholar Ortega Y Gasset puts it that the
man of antiquity, before he did anything, took a step
backwards, like the bull-fighter who leaps back to deliver
the mortal thrust. He searched the past for a pattern into
which he might slip as into a diving bell, and being thus at
once disguised and protected might rush upon his present
problem.

Classical mythology provided Jung with a lens through
which to distance himself and gain a perspective from which
to 'rush upon his present problem.' Upon reading Freud's
Traumdeutung Jung was so impressed that he likened the
recognition of the psychological power of the Oedipal myth
to 'that peculiar feeling which arises in us if, for example, in
the noise and tumult of a modern street we should come
across an ancient relic – the Corinthian capital of a walled-in
column, or a fragment of inscription.'

For nineteenth-century men like Freud and Jung the
classical world and classical mythology were still realities,
but filtered through the smoke of the industrial revolution
and modernity. Modern 'knowledge does not enrich us;

it removes us more and more from the mystic world in which we were once at home by right of birth,' Jung wrote, but he could not erase the lessons of modernization no matter how hard he tried. Since we can never really return to primitive innocence once we have eaten from the tree of scientific knowledge, our only salvation, Jung felt, is to integrate the archaic and the modern within our own consciousness. That was the task, begun and left unfinished by Goethe, Nietzsche, and Freud, which Jung undertook to complete.

Classical antiquity, world mythology, gnosticism and hermetic alchemy served Jung as Archimedian reference points, beyond the pale of modernity, from which to bear down on the mundane realities of modern life. With this Schopenhauerian vision, the present fell into perspective. Discounting the modern world as a temporary aberration, Jung could find solace in his historical and mythical fantasies and identifications. In the life-review process he undertook in dictating his memoirs, typically to a woman rather than a man, Jung concluded that 'I can only measure myself against the centuries . . . measured by the ideas of today it means nothing' (Jung, 1961, p. 6).

Jung's conversion experience at mid-life was to his own religion of the archetypes. Psychology became Mythology. Libido became Eros. Parental imago figures became archetypal structures. Beyond and behind the personal phenomenal world lay the eternal forms, the Platonic Schopenhauerian Idea. For Jung this act of 'seeing through' appearances to the underlying primordial forms and essential structures of the psyche was his act of 'divine service' in the tradition of his Protestant forbears. His 'calling' was to bring light into the darkness in order that 'the Creator may become conscious of His creation, and man conscious of himself' (Jung 1961).

Whereas Freud set out to unmask all the schemes and subterfuges of our souls, with his technique of amplification, Jung 'converted' psycho-analysis to psycho-synthesis. By re-mythologizing psychology Jung added a Christian mythic dimension to give meaning and context to individual lives. Freud, Jung felt, had remained on the level of natural history seeing human life as a war of all against all, an elaborate repetition of the story of evolution over millions of years. For Jung the history of the mind offered a different picture. He called the miracle of reflecting consciousness 'the second cosmogony.' Behind all the monstrous, apparently senseless biological turmoil, Jung felt that he divined an element of meaning.

> By virtue of his reflective faculties man is raised out of the animal world, and by his mind he demonstrates that nature has put a high premium precisely upon the development of consciousness. Through consciousness he takes possession of nature by recognizing the existence of the world and thus, as it were, confirming the Creator. (Jung, 1961)

In the end Jung agreed with the Protestant mystic Angelus Silesius who said:

> I know that without me God cannot live a moment;
> If I am destroyed He must give up the ghost.

Jung's metaphysics was deeply rooted in German romantic idealism and cosmic pantheism, children of the Pfarrhaus (parsonage), like Jung himself.

What was Jung, the man, like to meet 'face to face'? Professor Henry A. Murray (1962), who knew him as an old man, described him as follows:

> Jung was humble before the ineffable mystery of each variant self that faced him for the first time, as he sat at this desk, pipe in hand, with every faculty attuned, brooding on the portent of what was being said to him. And he never hesitated to acknowledge his perplexity in the presence of a strange and inscrutable phenomenon. He never hesitated to admit the provisional nature of the comments he had to make or to emphasize the difficulties and limitations of possible achievement in the future. 'Who-

ever comes to me,' he would say, 'takes his life in his hands.' The effect of such statements, the effect of his manner of delivering his avowals of uncertainty and suspense, was not to diminish but to augment the patient's faith in his physician's invincible integrity, as well as to make plain that the patient must take the burden of responsibility for whatever decisions he might make.

Certainly there had been scholars whose erudition was greater than Jung's, and poets who created more magical metaphors to convey their subjective experience. There have been other doctors and priests who were able to bring their entire body, mind, and soul to focus on the plight of the suffering person who came to them for help. But few have been 'so acutely perceptive – hour after hour, day after day – of the unique particularities of feeling, thought, and action manifested by the individual' confronting them (Murray, 1902). Few have been so penetrating and infallible in putting their fingers on the crux of their clients' dilemmas. Few were so imaginative in drawing from so vast a wealth of knowledge at the timely moment culling from their rich life experience whatever was most pertinent to the understanding of the problem at hand. Jung 'was such a master of apt and pithy utterance that he could transmute his understanding into words which at their best would memorably convey not only a new and startling revelation of the existential difficulty, but a clue to its solution, an intimation of the saving way, and the courage to embark on it' (ibid.).

In the words of one young man who went to Jung for the first time:

> Dr. Jung was the first, full-blooded, all-encompassing, spherical human being I had ever met and I knew of no fit standards, no adequate operations by which to measure his circumference and diameters. I had only the touch-stone of my peculiar tribulation to apply to his intelligence with the importunate demand that he interpret what I presumably knew best – myself. He proved more than

equal to this exacting test and within an hour my life was permanently set on a new course. In the next few days 'the great floodgates of the wonderworld swung open' and I experienced the unconscious in that immediate and moving way that cannot be drawn out of books. I came to see that my ongoing life was small adventure and the world as I had known it no conclusion. Instead of remaining framed by the standard judgements of my locality and time, I saw myself as the inheritor and potential bearer and promoter of mute historic forces struggling for emergence, consciousness, fulfillment, and communication. All this and more I owe to Dr. Jung. (ibid.)

Chapter 1
The emergence of adult developmental psychology

There was no explicit developmental psychology of personality through the life-span before the middle of the twentieth century. There was not even any systematic set of psychological data concerning the first half of anyone's life span. There were biographies, and, of course, there were works of fiction, but until quite recently there were no tested theories or models of psychological development covering the human life cycle. Even today the field of 'adult development' is in its infancy.

Before 1930 the psychology of personality development had scarcely moved beyond Shakespeare. His portrait of the seven ages of man expressed succinctly the image of the stages of life that prevails among most educated men to this day.

> All the world's a stage,
> And all the men and women merely players;
> They have their exits and their entrances,
> And one man in his time plays many parts,
> His acts being seven ages. At first the infant,
> Mewling and puking in the nurse's arms.
> Then the whining schoolboy, with his satchel,
> And shining morning face, creeping like a snail,
> Unwillingly to school. And then the lover,
> Sighing like a furnace, with a woeful ballad
> Made to his mistress' eyebrow. Then a soldier,
> Full of strange oaths and bearded like the pard,
> Jealous in honour, sudden and quick in quarrel,

Seeking the bubble reputation
Even in the cannon's mouth. And then the justice,
In fair round belly with good capon lin'd,
With eyes severe and beard of formal cut,
Full of wise saws and modern instances;
And so he plays his part. The sixth age shifts,
Into the lean and slipper'd pantaloon,
With spectacles on nose and pouch on side;
His youthful hose, well sav'd, a world too wide
For his shrunk shank, and his big manly voice,
Turning again toward childish treble, pipes
And whistles in his sound. Last scene of all,
That ends this strange eventful history,
Is second childishness and mere oblivion,
Sans teeth, sans eyes, sans taste, sans everything.
                                             (*As You Like It*, II vii)

The foundations for a developmental psychology of the personality were laid in the second quarter of the twentieth century by Carl Gustav Jung,[1] Charlotte Bühler and Fred Massarik (1968), Robert Havinghurst (1948), and Erik Erikson (1950). In contrast to most other psychologists they recognized that human development continues throughout the life cycle, and they argued that every person's life has a basic developmental structure because all lives are governed by common developmental principles. These early developmental psychologists sought to discover and analyze the developmental tasks every adult faces as he or she moves from one developmental phase to another through the life course. Their schemata of life stages and the developmental tasks related to them differed, but these psychologists shared the basic assumption that while each individual life has its own unique character, normal adult development follows a predictable patterned sequence of stages. Hence, this approach to personality development is called stage theory.

The period from 1850 to 1920 saw a good deal of empirical study of child and adolescent development. However, there was little attention to adulthood and later life. Psychologists assumed that personality was controlled by inheritance, therefore research focused on the description of the unfolding of inborn patterns. To the extent that the later periods of life were studied at all, this research was done under the rubrics of gerontology and geriatrics. The model employed was one of pathology not one of normal adult development. Until quite recently most persons calling themselves developmental psychologists were primarily interested in children and not really interested in life-span developmental psychology.

The serious study of normal adult development in American psychology was inaugurated by G. Stanley Hall early in the twentieth century. His book, *Adolescence*, published in 1904, became a standard text on the subject for many years. In this work he viewed the strains of the pre-adult years both in terms of physiological changes and in terms of adaptation to changing norms and expectations of the adult social world. Towards the end of his long career, Hall began to investigate the aging process. Finally in 1922 he published his book *Senescence: The Last Half of Life*, in which he presented an interpretation of the life course in terms of a theory of life stages.

Only in the 1920s and 1930s did psychologists begin to take seriously the influence of culture and the environment in shaping behavior. Some of these psychologists, the behaviorists, saw the personality as a *tabula rasa* on which the social environment could stamp almost any pattern of behavior. Others saw the personality as a pattern of behavior that emerged from the interaction of the human organism with its social environment. In this view the organism was considered to possess an active force that made demands on the social environment and was at the same time, at least to some extent, shaped by adaptation to its environment. Some members of this group, notably Charlotte Bühler, Robert Havinghurst, and Erik Erikson became interested in the life-span development of personality. Since then, the new field of life-span developmental psychology has emerged from the foundations laid by these pioneers.

Charlotte Bühler and self-realization theory

In the 1920s in Berlin, the neo-Freudian psychoanalyst Karen Horney began to elaborate and expand a conception of the personality as teleologically directed towards self-realization. In her view, neurosis resulted from a person's losing the thread of his or her own inner guiding direction, from becoming too concerned to please others and forgetting their own deepest satisfactions and needs (Horney, 1950). Horney rebelled against Freud's model of the personality subdivided into id, ego, and superego. Instead she thought holistically of the whole person as a total *Gestalt* to be understood as a whole rather than as a system of conflicting parts. Horney's self-realization model had a great influence on a number of other psychologists including Charlotte Bühler, Abraham Maslow, and Fritz Perls.

Whereas most developmental psychologists have emphasized the organizing and guiding role of the ego in human development, Bühler judged that the ego is often only a manifestation of the individual reality interests and does not adequately represent the personality as a whole with its sometimes reality-transcendent orientation and its unconscious depths. She, therefore, spoke of the real self as the center of the personality. Bühler defines the real self as 'a core system which organizes, selects and integrates the multitude of motivational trends' (Bühler and Massarik, 1968) in a self-realizing direction. This notion of self-realization underlies her conception of *The Course of Human Life* (1968), originally published in 1933, her major book on life-span developmental psychology.

In formulating her theory, Bühler did not use the Freudian model because she felt that

> Freud's system leaves no room for the fundamental role
> of creativity, for a primarily positive reality, anticipated
> and accepted as an opportunity rather than as a hindrance,
> and for a conscience that is rooted in the self instead of in
> social roles (Bühler and Massarik, 1968, p. 19).

She was critical of ego-psychology because she felt that the ego may pursue ambitions or false values and may be responsible for a person's defecting from his real self. Any personality guided by considerations solely on the ego level was bound to be 'lacking in depth because its self-direction does not come from the core of the personality.'

Bühler was convinced from her studies of many biographies as well as clinical cases that at the deepest levels of the personality there is a core self which is oriented to purpose and meaning. Her term for a life that is directed toward fulfillment of an abiding purpose was 'self-determination'. She evaluated the degree of development of persons in terms of their autonomy, authenticity, and the congruity between their values and their actual lives. Her normative theory of development was quite remarkable in the scientific milieu of her time when most psychologists were still committed to the so-called value-free objectivity of the sciences. In viewing human life as directed toward purposeful, meaningful living, Bühler approached closely to the work of Carl Jung and anticipated the existential psychology of Rollo May and Viktor Frankl.

Robert J. Havinghurst and socialization theory

During the period 1935–50 a group of psychologists worked inter-actively first in New York City and then in Chicago and in Berkeley on studies of child development. The members of this group shared a dynamic or organismic theory of personality development. In their staff discussions they sought to combine awareness of the drive toward growth of the individual with the demands, constraints, and opportunities provided by the social environment – the family, school, peer group, and community. They began to speak of a series of life adjustment tasks to be achieved by the growing person in relation to his environment. Eventually the term developmental task came into use in writings of several members of this group during the 1940s.

Robert J. Havinghurst, one of the members of this group, started to teach courses in child and adolescent development at the University of Chicago in 1941. He published his lecture material in 1948 and this work came into wide use as a standard text in the field. In this work he divided the life cycle into the following periods: (1) early childhood – birth to 5 or 6; (2) middle childhood – 5 or 6 to 12 or 13; (3) adolescence – 12 or 13 to 18; (4) early adulthood – 18 to 35; (5) middle adulthood – 35 to 60; (6) later maturity – 60 and over. Havinghurst's theory is one primarily based on biological development and social expectations which change through the life span and give direction, force, and substance to the development of personality.

In order to have a scientifically fruitful and viable area of study known as life-span personality development, Havinghurst suggests that the following conditions should be met:

1 Researchers should work with an organismic theory of personality, assuming the existence of something like a self-actualizing tendency.

2 The personality theory should assume that the biological organism interacts with the social and physical environment, seeking satisfaction of needs and drives.

3 Researchers should look for evidence of change of personality at all age levels.

4 Researchers should concern themselves with *live* problems – including controversial ones (Havinghurst, 1973).

Havinghurst suggested some of the following problem areas that would enrich life-span personality research: the study of career changes in relation to personality, where the changes take place in middle age; study of the perceptions of aging and of old age by the self, the family, and the wider community; study of personality changes associated with marked change in physical vigor and health; study of the relations between personality and favorite leisure activities; study of the attitudes toward death held by people of various ages and personality types; and study of the correlates of senility (Havinghurst, 1973).

Erik Erikson and psychosocial development theory

In 1950 Erikson published *Childhood and Society* which was destined to become one of the most influential books of the century on personality development. Erikson presented a theory of personality development through the life span, with a set of eight psychosocial tasks, each of which dominated the individual at a certain stage in his development. Erikson's (1950) psychosocial tasks and their age periods are:

Basic trust vs. mistrust	Birth to 1 year
Autonomy vs. shame, doubt	1–6
Initiative vs. guilt	6–10
Industry vs. inferiority	10–14
Identity vs. role confusion	Adolescence: 14–20
Intimacy vs. isolation	Early adulthood: 20–40
Generativity vs. stagnation	Middle adulthood: 40–65
Ego integrity vs. despair	Later adulthood: 65–

Erikson started with a major interest in development during the first twenty years of life, but found his curiosity and psychological activity carrying him on into the study of adulthood. His studies of Luther (1958) and Gandhi (1969) led him to concentrate his attention on adult development and the developmental tasks of adulthood.

Whereas Freud saw the personality as structured and set in early childhood, Erikson sees the personality in its essence as always developing. This led Erikson to regard the life cycle as a continuing series of steps each presenting possibilities for new growth, in contrast to Freud's view of adulthood as a mere unfolding of events whose direction had already been determined in childhood. In Erikson's view, psychosocial development proceeds by 'crises': decisive turning points where a shift one way or another is unavoidable. He underscored this developmental crisis aspect by assigning double terms to each life stage, emphasizing that basic conflicts are never fully resolved but continue to recur in later life.

A new life task presents a crisis whose outcome can be

successful graduation, or alternatively, an impairment of the life cycle which will aggravate future crises, . . . Each crisis prepares the next, as one step leads to another; and each crisis lays one more cornerstone for the adult personality (Erikson, 1958, p. 254).

As we proceed through the life course, development becomes more and more complex. A restructuring of all previous identifications occurs which often means having to fight some earlier battles over again. When a later crisis is severe, earlier crises are likely to be revived. Despite the identity crisis having been resolved in adolescence, later stresses can precipitate its renewal. Furthermore, all eight stages are present throughout the life cycle.

The crisis of young adulthood concerns intimacy vs. isolation. If it is resolved favorably it results in the capacity to love. The crisis of the middle years, which begins around forty, centers on generativity vs. stagnation and if resolved favorably results in the ability to care. 'Generativity' applies beyond ones own family to caring for other persons and for ones products and ideas.

Erikson believes that 'adult man is so constituted as to *need to be needed* lest he suffer the mental deformation of self-absorption in which he becomes his own infant and pet.' Teaching is a good example of generativity and illustrates the way in which the life stages interlock within a total life cycle. It connects the adult, the child, and the culture. The final stage of life pits ego integrity vs. despair and if resolved successfully leads to wisdom. Fortified by matured judgment the wise man is able to accept his 'one and only life cycle as something that had to be and that, by necessity, permitted of no substitutions' (Erikson, 1950, p. 268). Despite being aware of different life-styles, the wise man defends the dignity of his own. 'Only such integrity can balance the despair of the knowledge that a limited life is coming to a conscious conclusion, only such wholeness can transcend the petty disgust of feeling finished and passed by' (ibid.). Because Erikson sees the

life cycle as a circular interlocking bond between the generations, the successful resolution of this final crisis is of vital
importance. Infantile trust, the first ego strength, depends
on adult integrity, the last ego strength. As they rotate,
the generations nourish and enrich each other when a culture
respects the old as much as the young.

Daniel Levinson and life structure theory

The most comprehensive theory of adult development
produced so far in this very young field is that of Daniel
Levinson and his colleagues at Yale University. They are
the only group to have studied the male mid-life period
in depth and to have placed it in a life-cycle context. Levinson's data are limited to men; we do not yet know if the
same analyses apply to women.

Levinson's conceptual framework, which encompasses
'the periods in the evolution of the individual life structure,'
is broader than previous theories which focused on stages
in ego development, cognitive development, moral development or some other aspect of personality functioning. It
is the most holistic general developmental theory now
in use. His theory is not a blueprint specifying a single
normal course that everyone must follow. Its function
is to indicate the developmental tasks that everyone must
work on in successive periods, and the infinitely varied form
that such work can take in different individuals living under
different conditions' (Levinson, Darrow, Klein, Levinson,
and McKee, 1978). Rather than imposing a template of
uniformity, his theory offers a theme upon which each individual life may be viewed as playing a series of variations.

The central organizing concept in Levinson's theory
is that of the 'individual life structure' which he sees as
evolving through a relatively orderly sequence during the
adult years. 'It consists of a series of alternating stable
[structure-building] periods' (Levinson et al., 1978, p. 49).
The basic task of every stable period is to build a life structure. The way people do this is through making certain key

choices, usually relating to career, marriage, family and the like. They then form a life structure around these choices and pursue goals and values within this structure. A 'transitional period' terminates an existing life structure and creates the possibility for a new one. The primary tasks of these transitional periods are to question and reappraise the existing structure 'to explore possibilities for change in self and world and to move towards commitment to the crucial choices that form the basis for a new life structure in the ensuing stable period' (ibid.). The task of such a developmental transition is to terminate a time in one's life: to accept the losses the termination entails; to review and evaluate the past; to decide which aspects of the past to keep and which to reject; and to consider one's wishes and possibilities for the future. In transition periods one is suspended between past and future, struggling to overcome the gap that separates them. While much from the past can be used as a basis for the future, much must also be disregarded and renounced usually with some attendant mourning. Transition times are times of crisis – and of opportunity.

I find Levinson's notion of the 'individual life structure' very useful for interpreting the patterns of adult development in individual lives. It gives us a way of examining the lived experience of a person in such a way that we consider both self and world in interaction. This concept of life structure offers an analytic framework for biography, the interpretation of a life. Levinson prides himself on this, acknowledging 'we are engaged here in one form of biography.'

Levinson and his colleagues began with the question 'Is there a normal process of individual development in adulthood?' They were particularly interested in understanding the processes of change in individual lives. They wanted to know why transition periods like the mid-life period lead to a constriction in some men's lives and an expansion in others. Though they began from issues related to the mid-life crisis, soon their work led them to ask questions about how adult life evolves over time, and they concluded that a number of age-linked developmental periods exist between eighteen and forty-five.

Levinson and his colleagues divide the adult life course into several major eras: early adulthood (20–40), middle adulthood (40–60), and late adulthood (60 and over). Within each era Levinson distinguishes several periods (See Figure 1).

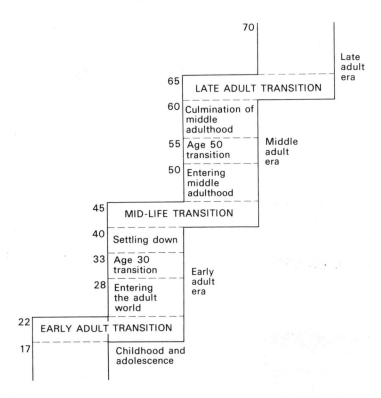

Figure 1   *Developmental periods over the life course.*
Source: Levinson et al., 1978.

Leaving the family (18–22)
This is the transition between adolescence and full entry into the adult world. In this period a young man is busy creating a basis for adult life. He is usually half in and half out of the

family, but trying to separate himself from their support and authority. This involves moving out of the family home, becoming financially independent, and assuming new roles that make him more autonomous, and responsible. The process of separation from parents continues over the entire life cycle and is never fully completed, according to Levinson. However there are changes in the kind and degree of our attachment to our parents during the life course. In this early adult transition, one must give up some aspects of the pre-adult self and world while internalizing other aspects as a groundwork for adult development.

The second major task of this transition period is to form a basis for living in the adult world. At this time a young man's knowledge, values, and aspirations for a particular style of adult life may be rather ambiguous or colored by extravagant fantasies. He needs to obtain further training and to learn more about himself and the world. College and/or military service provide the institutional settings where many young men begin to separate from their families of origin and begin inner and outer developmental work necessary to complete the early adult transition.

Entering the adult world (22-28)

Like all developmental transitions the early adult transition is followed by a more stable period in which a new life structure must be built. A young man now tries to establish an occupation and to form more mature friendships and sexual relationships – including, perhaps, marriage. The developmental task of this period is to arrive at a preliminary sense of himself as an adult and to fashion an initial life structure based on his interests and goals. This is a time of exploration and for making some important choices.

Levinson suggests that many, but not all, young men enter this period with a dream of their personal future. Often this dream relates to their work. A young man may dream of becoming president of the company, or of writing a great novel. This dream, Levinson feels, is vital for further growth. Without it, life can be oppressive or empty. In later years reactivation of this guiding image or dream and concern with its failure may become a major developmental issue. Major shifts around forty are often stimulated by the feeling that one has betrayed or compromised one's dream.

Levinson and his colleagues discovered that having a mentor during this period is highly correlated with a man's future growth – and his success. Eight to fifteen years older, this mentor may be a teacher, boss, editor, or experienced co-worker who represents a level of achievement to which the younger man aspires. He invites the younger man into his world, shows him around, and – most crucial – gives his blessing to the dream. In this way the mentor not only helps foster the younger man's development, but also re-inforces his sense of manhood. In addition, Levinson found, a man often relies on the 'loved woman' during this period to give her blessing to his dream and help facilitate his entry into adulthood.

Age 30 transition (28–32)
During this period a man generally questions whether he should continue in his chosen occupation, or make a change while he still has a chance. While most men remain in the occupation initially chosen and remain in existing marriage relationships, there are many occupational and marital shifts at this time. Toward the end of this transition a man's thoughts focus on the future.

With the termination of the age 30 transition, the preparatory phase of adulthood is completed. A man is now an adult. He is committed to a new life structure through which he will operate for the next eight to ten years. This new life structure, which Levinson calls 'settling down,' is built in the next period. It provides the framework for a young man to attain his aspirations during his thirties.

Settling down (32–39)
During this period a man usually makes deeper commitments to his work and his family. He 'joins the tribe' as Levinson puts it. A man has devoted himself in the novice adult phase

to creating a foundation. He now begins to climb the career ladder. The more he has already accomplished the higher the level on which he can now start his personal career-building enterprise. The occupation chosen usually provides a rough timetable for reaching various levels of advancement. The early settling down phase is devoted to building a life around our initial choices. It is a time for making one's niche in society, defining an enterprise, getting on with the work. During the settling down period a young man enters a career world in which he is a junior member. He seeks to advance in the enterprise, to climb the ladder and become a senior member of that world. In this period his sense of wellbeing as a person will depend upon his evaluation of how far and how fast he is moving toward these goals.

Late settling down: becoming one's own man (36–41)
The man's primary developmental task in this period is to accomplish the goals of settling down, to advance sufficiently on his ladder, to become a senior member of his enterprise, to speak more clearly with his own voice, to have a greater measure of authority, and to become less dependent on other individuals and institutions in his life. The wish for independence leads a man to do what he alone considers most essential, regardless of consequence; yet the wish for affirmation in society makes him sensitive to the response of others and susceptible to their influence.

During this period a man may have a sense of being held back – of being oppressed by others and restrained by his own conflicts and inhibitions. These concerns reflect external realities and internal processes. External circumstances during these years are frequently restrictive and damaging to self-esteem. As a man advances, he comes in closer contact with senior men who have their territories to protect. Organizations are often rigid and restrictive of personal initiative and development. On the other hand, the wish for affirmation, approval, and advancement make men especially vulnerable to social pressures and inner feelings of anxiety. The urgency of the desires for manhood bring about the resurgence of the little boy in the adult. Levinson believes that the activation of the boyish self during the late thirties is part of normal psychosocial development, and considers intensification of the boy/man conflict a positive step forward creating the possibility of resolving the conflict at a higher level.

During this period mentor relationships are likely to be particularly stormy and vulnerable. Termination of close ties with a mentor now is often a mutually painful process. He is not only giving up his current mentor but he is out-growing the readiness to be the protégé of any older person.

The mid-life transition (39–42)

When a man experiences a developmental crisis in the late thirties, it stems from the feeling that he cannot accomplish the tasks of becoming one's own man; he cannot advance sufficiently on his chosen ladder; cannot gain the affirmation, independence and seniority he wants; cannot be his own man in the terms defined by his current life structure. At around forty a new period gets under way which Levinson calls the mid-life transition. The task here is to come to terms with the past and to prepare for the future, and to take steps toward the initiation of middle adulthood.

For the majority of men this period evokes tumultuous struggles within the self and with the external world. Every aspect of their lives comes into question. They are full of recriminations against themselves and others. They cannot go on as before, but need time to choose a new path or modify the old one. The process of reappraisal activates unconscious conflicts, anxiety, guilt, the dependencies, animosities, and vanities of earlier years that keep a man from examining the real issues at mid-life. They make it difficult for him to modify an oppressive life structure. 'Every genuine reappraisal must be agonizing,' Levinson says, 'because it challenges the illusions and vested inter-ests on which the existing structure is based' (1978).

Why is there a crisis at mid-life? 'We need developmental transitions in adulthood partly because no life structure can permit the living out of all aspects of the self' (Levinson *et al.*, 1968, p. 200). In making a life structure I make choices, selecting one option and rejecting others. Every life structure necessarily gives high priority to certain aspects of the self and neglects or minimizes other aspects. At mid-life neglected parts of the self urgently seek self expression. A man hears voices of an identity prematurely rejected, a love lost or not pursued, possibilities set aside to become what he is now.

Restabilization: entering middle adulthood (45–50)
In most cases a man is not able to form a stable life structure at the start of middle adulthood. A man stays in this period as long as his predominant development task is to create a satisfactory structure. A man has had his time for reapprais-ing, exploring, testing choices, and creating the basis for a new life. Now he must make his choices and begin forming a new life structure. The life structure that emerges in the middle forties varies greatly in its suitability for the self. Some men simply don't make it. Others form a life structure that is viable in the world but poorly connected with the self. Others are less tyrannized by the ambitions, passions, and illusions of youth. They can be more deeply attached to others yet more separate and centered in the self.

By his late forties a man has formed an initial life structure for middle adulthood. Where does he go from there? Levin-son and his colleagues do not really know. They postulate that there is an age 50 transition followed by building a second middle adult structure, but this is conjecture. Because their data gave out at this point, they were not able to work out the phases of later life development. Their work is strongest on early adulthood through the mid-life transition.

Nevitt Sanford and holistic theory

Over the years various psychologists have set forth positive goals for personality development. One of the most innova-tive of these has been Nevitt Sanford. As a student of Henry A. Murray, Sanford views personality as a highly complex 'vast and intricate architecture.' He argues that it is a mistake to think that problems or functions of the personality can be neatly separated in living persons, for every personality is a whole, a totality, a living *Gestalt*. Like Goldstein (1939), Maslow (1954), and Jung (1972a), Sanford conceives of the human organism as being a self-reflecting, self-regulating and, at least partially, self-determining system. Furthermore, every person lives and develops in a social system and cultural context; therefore personality development must be understood with a view to these contexts. In other words, Sanford emphasizes the wholeness of personality and the interconnectedness of the parts within the whole as well as the relation of wholes (such as the personality) to other wholes (such as the culture and social system).

Perhaps Sanford's most important contribution to adult development theory is his theory of personality development throughout the life cycle. In a recent essay entitled 'Notes Toward a General Theory of Personality Development at Eighty or Any Old Age' (1981) Sanford attempted to analyze what makes developmental change take place. In his view, there are two ways in which development occurs: challenge and self-insight. Theoretically, personality development may occur at any age. It is a matter of helping the person find the stimulation for change in behavior and to achieve the self-insight necessary to the integration of these changes within the personality. However, as adults become increasingly committed to social roles, relationships, and responsibilities, it becomes increasingly difficult to find stimulus situations that can induce changes in behavior. Furthermore, adults still labor under a burden of unconscious structures built up in childhood or adolescence.

Sanford has found evidence that the sets of situational variables surrounding personality development are subject to alteration later in life. When the responsibilities of family life and career have been reduced, structures of habit and life pattern needed less for defensive purposes are more easily demolished or may crumble on their own. On the other hand, in some cases when this does not happen there will be increased rigidity in older persons.

The essence of Sanford's theory is that a developmental change in personality – at any age beyond childhood – occurs not through challenge *or* self-insight, considered as separate or successive processes, but *interaction* of the two. His theory may be summed up in the following general formulation:

1 For a change in personality to occur there must be a change in behavior.

2 Change in behavior depends upon the presence of an appropriate and effective challenge, one that is sufficient to upset equilibrium but not so extreme as to induce regression, that is to say, not too severe in an objective sense and not beyond the limits of the individual's adaptive capacities (ego strength).

3 In childhood and adolescence there are usually challenges in abundance but for adults the presentation of an effective challenge will ordinarily require a change in the person's general situation – in the social roles, relationships, responsibilities. and reward systems that structure his life.

4 A challenge must be experienced as such, and it must be accepted, if it is to induce durable change in behavior. Much of our general knowledge about the succession of developments in personality is based on the fact that we learn from experience and on the fact that it is possible within limits to predict when given experiences are likely to occur. However it is the individual's subjective definition of the situation that he responds to and if he is able to transform objectively new situations into equivalents of what he has experienced before, change in behavior may not be expected.

5 Steps can be taken to prevent the projection on to new situations of psychological content from the past, to overcome resistance to the assimilation of knowledge and to consideration of alternative ways of behaving and to connect new stimuli with inner needs and potentialities.

6 Personality development in adults requires self-examination aimed at self-insight. No amount of situation or

behavior changing will lead to personality development in adults if it is unaccompanied by conscious self-reflection. Sanford warns that the strategies and interventions of psychologists can be dehumanizing and amount to little more than manipulation if the person involved does not understand what is happening and is not encouraged to think about it in relation to the self. He concludes by noting that all the above conditions and processes are necessary to bring about developmental change in the adult personality.

In contrast to classical psychoanalytic theory, Sanford does not see the pattern of personality development set forever in childhood. Development occurs throughout the life cycle as a response to challenges in the person's environment. If personality exists in a kind of equilibrium with the contemporary environment, then changes in the environment may produce changes in the personality.

Carl Gustav Jung and individuation theory

In later parts of this work Jung's theory and contributions to adult developmental psychology will be discussed in detail, so I will only touch on these matters very briefly here. The prevailing view of Jung's work among developmental psychologists, at least until very recently, has been that it 'represented more of a philosophy of life than a theory of life-span development' (Havinghurst, 1973, p. 19). Despite Jung's numerous suggestive ideas on adult development, he did not attract many disciples among developmentalists probably because his basic worldview and philosophical and methodological assumptions differed radically from those of mainstream Western experimental and developmental psychology. This makes comparison and contrast of Jung with other adult developmental psychologists difficult.

Although Jung did not conceptualize his approach to the psyche as phenomenological, by comparing and contrasting the works of Jung with those of Husserl, Gurwitsch, Scheler, Heidegger, Schutz, Sartre, and Merleau-Ponty, a case can be made for interpreting Jung's analysis of the psyche as being a proto-phenomenology of consciousness. From this point of view the Jungian 'Self' may be seen as Being (*Dasein*), the ground and horizon of our experience, the context for the contents of consciousness and the unconscious.

Like William James, whom Jung knew personally, and whom he admired enormously, Jung was a radical empiricist, cataloging and describing the phenomena of the psychic world and everything that appeared on his mind screen without prejudging it. His essay on 'The Real and the Sur-real' (1972a) bears comparison with Alfred Schutz's essay 'On Multiple Realities' (1970).

In his *Principles of Psychology* (Vol. II, Chapter 21), William James showed that there are several orders of reality, probably an infinite number in fact, each with its own special style of existence. He called them 'subuniverses' of meaning and mentioned as examples: the world of physical things (our paramount reality), the world of science, the worlds of mythology and religion, the world of the 'idols of the tribe,' the worlds of individual opinions, and the world of madness. 'Each world,' James maintained, '*while it is attended to*, is real after its own fashion; only the reality lapses with the attention.' In other words, 'reality' refers to whatever is related to our emotional and active life. Whatever excites and stimulates our interest is real. Thus, for James and Jung the objects of dream and fantasy life were just as 'real' as the objects of the so-called 'real' physical world. Jung even went so far as to argue that the psyche was not only 'real,' but objective as well. 'In contrast to the subjectivism of the conscious mind, the unconscious is objective, manifesting itself mainly in the form of contrary feelings, fantasies, emotions, impulses, and dreams, none of which one makes oneself, but which come upon one objectively' (Jung, 1970, p. 291).

It is worthwhile to detail some of the qualities in Jung's work that has prevented its receiving the attention that I believe it deserves. Jung's obscure prose style, his admitted belief in spirits, his visions and his intense interest in occult and psychic phenomena, metaphysics and mysticism, as well as his emphasis on the development of the deeper self rather than the ego have kept him out of the mainstream of life-span developmental psychology as practiced today, with its emphasis on ego development and tasks of adaptation to the external environment. I believe that Jung was ahead of his time, and that with the recent development of trans-personal psychology and systems theory psychologists of the next generation will be more able than their predecessors to see the value in Jung's ideas and to build on them.

Jean Piaget echoed the prevailing attitude of most developmental psychologists towards Jung when he commented that

> Jung has an amazing capacity for construction, but a certain contempt for logic and rational activity, which he contracted through daily contact with mythical and symbolic thought, has made him inclined to be content with too little in the way of proof. The better to understand the realities of which he speaks, he adopts an anti-rationalistic attitude, and the surprising comparisons of which he has the secret cannot fail sometimes to disturb the critical reader (Piaget, 1962, p. 212).

Things are changing, however. 'Today many psychologists dedicated to the idea of adult growth are turning for inspiration to Swiss psychiatrist C. G. Jung' (Mayer, 1978, p. 85). In his recent study of *The Seasons of a Man's Life*, Daniel Levinson and his colleagues acknowledged Jung as 'the father of the modern study of adult development' (Levinson *et al.*, 1978, p. 4). He found the notions of early and middle adulthood 'implicit' in Jung's work, and he acknowledged the inspiration he drew from Jung's individuation theory for his own analysis of the male mid-life crisis. Levinson utilized Jung's archetypal theory in his work, as well, and indicated that 'under favorable developmental conditions, it is possible at mid-life to begin giving more attention to the archetypal unconscious, the inner source of self-definition, wisdom, and satisfaction' (1978, p. 37). In my opinion, Jung's influence on adult developmental psychology, like the field itself, is only now emerging and will be growing in the future.

Chapter 2
The making of a scientist

Early adulthood is the time when most men establish themselves and make their contribution to the survival of the
species: begetting and raising children, maintaining a marriage
and family, and producing for the welfare of themselves,
their family and their community or tribe. Within this period
a man normally moves from being a novice adult through a
series of steps to the point where he can assume a more
'senior' position in work, family, and community. Jung did
just this. Through disciplined hard work he overcame his
Oedipal ties and established himself in the world of medicine
rising to the top with remarkable skill in a matter of a few
years. He was lucky to find a career early in his life that
both fulfilled many of his own inner needs and contributed
to his society. It is my purpose in this chapter to trace and
analyze this ascent from youth through the novice adult
phase to seniority and mastery.

High above the rooftops of the old city stand the two
tall towers of the ancient cathedral of Basel. Carl Gustav
Jung grew up on the outskirts of Basel in the shadow of
the cathedral and the city. The tall towers of the cathedral,
visible from his village home on the Rhine, embodied for him
his own roots and family traditions. One tower stood for
the traditions of theology and religion from which his father
and his maternal ancestors had earned their living as ministers of the Swiss Reformed Church. The other tower stood
for the traditions of science and medicine, personified for
Jung in the life and work of his paternal grandfather and

namesake who reformed and revitalized the medical faculty and the university in the early nineteenth century. In his own career as a scholar-physician and psychotherapist, Jung blended the two traditions of medical science and theology, cure of body and cure of soul, consciously continuing the work of both sides of his ancestral heritage and integrating them.

There were many polarities of Jung's life and character. One day he was to build his psychological theory on the principle of reconciliation of the opposites. Already as a young man Jung thought of himself as being two people. In his memoirs he recalled:

> Somewhere deep in the background I always knew that I was two persons. One was the son of my parents, who went to school and was less intelligent, attentive, hardworking, decent and clean than many other boys. The other was grown-up – old in fact – skeptical, mistrustful, remote from the world of men, but close to nature, the earth, the sun, the moon, the weather, all living creatures, and above all close to the night, to dreams, and to whatever 'god' worked directly in him (Jung, 1961, p. 44).

Beside the world of the first personality, the schoolboy, there existed within Jung another world, the magical, mysterious realm of what he called the second personality. It was 'like a temple in which anyone who entered was transformed and overpowered by a vision of the whole cosmos' (Jung, 1961, p. 45). Here lived 'the Other,' his *daimon* or spirit guide, his Higher Self, who knew the Pleroma, the *Urgrund*, the God behind the gods, the personal and the transpersonal aspects of divinity. When he felt the power of the second personality come over him, Jung later wrote, 'I knew I was worthy of myself, that I was my true self' (Jung, 1961, p. 45). As a boy he liked to walk alone in the mountains or along the Swiss lakes or the Rhine. Here in nature he easily passed from the insecurity of the first personality to the serenity of the second. As he grew older and approached young adulthood, Jung felt forced to choose between these two personalities. Gradually the second was pushed into the background and he invested himself more and more in the first and the world of his ego goals.

This is the way Jung interpreted his experience of his divided self. Phenomenologically, I have no quarrel with this schema, but analytically it seems important to point out a more objective framework. Whereas Jung, with the hindsight of age, seemed to feel that his second personality was more profound and morally superior to his first, which he identified with his ego and its goals, I want to suggest that the perspectives of each of these, as well as other subpersonalities within Jung, had equal validity and served to enhance and round out his adult development. More specifically, I am not convinced that Jung's second personality was really the voice of his deeper Self; it appears to me to be simply another face of the ego, equally socialized and conditioned in its own way. It bespoke rather conventional Swiss morality and Jung's Swiss Protestant and pietist upbringing.

On the other hand, even if this was the voice of Jung's deeper Self, it seems to me that following Jung's own theory he might have balanced the voice of his ego consciousness (first personality) against that of other internal figures, complexes, or archetypal structures rather than identified it with the unconscious or allowed himself to be dominated by it. In fact, sometimes the inner Self can be just as ruthlessly selfish and even as self-destructive as any other complex. There is good evidence for this in Jung's own autobiography in which he revealed how much he felt himself to be the hapless victim of his own 'daimon of creativity' which he felt had 'ruthlessly had its way with me' (Jung, 1961, p. 356). In his old age, Jung identified with the archetype of the sage which he retrospectively read back into his youthful 'second personality.' He thereby failed to recognize the value of his own young adult *persona*, his 'first personality.'

Jung's split personality was reflected in his difficulties in choosing a vocation. On the one hand he was attracted to science because its truths were based on empirically demonstrable facts. On the other hand he was fascinated with everything that had to do with philosophy and religion, which appeared to his second personality, which missed the philosophical and religious dimension in science. What appealed to Jung in science were the concrete facts viewed in their contextual background. Philosophy and comparative religion, on the other hand, opened the doors to exciting spiritual problems and raised fundamental questions regarding the meaning of life. Though philosophy offered a mythic meaningful framework for Jung's deeper Self, his ego consciousness symbolized by the first personality preferred the hard facts of science (Jung, 1961, pp. 72–87).

In the end, after much inner turmoil, Jung opted for the natural sciences and enrolled in medical school. He continued to read Kant, Schopenhauer, and Nietzsche for his own edification, but peer pressure and economic necessity pushed him to abandon his adolescent love of philosophy and to 'grow up' and adopt the hard-nosed attitude of science as his way of adapting to the adult world (ibid., p. 87).

In his memoirs Jung says that a series of dreams helped him to make his decision for science as against philosophy, religion, or archeology. From these dreams he decided that he must get to know living nature, as Goethe had done. He wanted to understand 'the world in which we live and the things around us' (ibid., p. 86). If dreams helped him make the decision for science, it was purely practical considerations that led him to choose medicine. His father was ill and could not support him. Like Freud, though he would have preferred to study pure natural science, Jung became a medical student in order to enter a career in which he could support himself and his family.

From his account in his memoirs, it appears that Jung approached his introductory psychiatry courses with prejudice, thinking that the subject was a waste of time. He had also heard tales of the conditions of life in asylums that repelled him. He seems to have shared the layman's view that mental disease was a hopeless affair. Despite his prejudices, however, in a relatively short time Jung decided to give up his opportunity to continue his studies of internal medicine, in which he had been offered an assistantship, and to study psychiatry.

Apparently what changed his mind toward psychiatry was his encounter with Krafft-Ebing's standard psychiatry textbook. When he opened the book he said to himself, 'Well, now let's see what a psychiatrist has to say for himself' (Jung, 1961, p. 108). Beginning with the preface he read: 'It is probably due to the peculiarity of the subject and its incomplete state of development that psychiatric textbooks are stamped with a more or less *subjective character.*' Later he noted that the author called the psychoses 'diseases of the personality.' His heart leapt. His excitement was so intense that he stood up and paced around the room as he continued to read. He did not find the answers he was looking for in that book, but he did find his vocation:

> Here alone the two currents of my interest could flow together and in a united stream dig their own bed. Here was the empirical field common to biological and spiritual facts, which I had everywhere sought and nowhere found. Here at last was the place where the collision of nature and spirit became a reality (Jung, 1961, p. 109).

Here his 'united double nature' had found its true and proper field of action and reflection.

What seems to have appealed most to Jung about this text was the idea that the book itself was in part the subjective confession of its author. 'With his specific prejudice, with the totality of his being, he stands behind the objectivity of his experiences and responds to the "disease of the personality" with the whole of his personality' (Jung, 1961, p. 109). Jung concluded that a good psychiatrist must personally confront the diseases of the personality within himself if he wants to have any hope of really assisting his patients. He felt challenged. Here was what he was looking for, the field where he could make his mark. Of that he was certain.

For his doctoral dissertation Jung chose to write about 'The psychology and pathology of so-called occult phenomena' (Jung, 1970a). Although he included several clinical hospitalized cases in his study, the major portion of his dissertation was devoted to an analysis of the utterances and behavior of a young medium. During his college years he had assisted at a number of seances conducted by his cousin, Helene Preiswerk. The phenomena he observed during the seances and the changes in the personality of the girl while she was in a somnambulistic trance fascinated him. He became convinced that there was some kind of a world behind consciousness and that the medium was in contact with this 'other world.' As the science of the time seemed to offer to him no satisfying explanation of these 'so-called occult phenomena,' Jung turned to German romantic philosophy and to the literature of spiritualism. From Schopenhauer, Jung got the idea of a universal will that might be purposive. This conception helped him understand his cousin 'because I thought I could trace clearly in her signs of something working the unconscious toward a goal' (Jung, 1925, p. 4). From this time on Jung began to think of the unconscious as something real and purposive. He turned to psychiatry to unravel the mystery of the unconscious.

Jung found the possibility of the existence of psychic phenomena and a psychic dimension extremely appealing. It added a further dimension to his life. He speculated on the relationship between dreams and ghosts. He read widely in Swedenborg and Jacob Boehme, and in German romantic literature. He discovered Kant's 'Dreams of a Spirit Seer' just at the right moment and soon afterward read Karl Duprel who had evaluated these ideas philosophically and psycho-logically. Soon he was immersed in other romantic writers – Görres, Eschenmayer, Passavant, Justinus Kerner – and other key figures of the romantic revival in the nineteenth century (Jung, 1961, p. 99). And of course there was Goethe's *Faust*, which he returned to again and again throughout his life. Perhaps the hallucinations of Margaret in prison, tortured by guilt which drove her mad, increased Jung's fascination with hallucinatory experience, demonic visions, and mental illness. In any case, Jung's experience of altered state of consciousness in his cousin inspired him to study these matters more deeply and he continued to study psychic and para-normal experiences for the rest of his life.

In his dissertation Jung interpreted the development of the personality of Helene Preiswerk as follows. First she began speaking of ghosts. Soon after this she made contact with the 'ghost' of her grandfather, Samuel Preiswerk (who was also Jung's grandfather). Then she made contact with Goethe and gradually more and more people came into her fantasies. Finally she developed Ivenes, the most significant subpersonality with which she identified herself. Jung felt that 'it was as though each of the great personages had left a deposit in her out of which grew her greater personality' (Jung, 1925, p. 9). He spoke of this new higher self as a 'mediatory symbol,' thus anticipating the direction he was later to take when he encouraged his patients to develop such symbols, which he then called a 'transcendent function.'

What seems most striking to a reader of the dissertation and Jung's account of these seance experiments in his memoirs is the contrast in tone. Perhaps the ascerbic scientific style of the dissertation was demanded by his director, but I think that Jung actually cultivated this style to give the impression of being more objective about the case than he actually was. It seems almost as if he were trying hard to dissociate himself from any sympathy for these 'so called occult' experiences. Once again we see him suppressing the second personality for the sake of identifying more fully with his scientific persona, the first personality. He attempted to distance himself from his material by calling altered states of consciousness 'pathological.' From his memoirs it seems clear that Jung was actually very interested in the 'case' of Helene Preiswerk because in her, as in his mother, he saw the same dual nature that he had discovered in himself. Like Goethe, who wrote *The Sorrows of Young Werther* thereby throwing off his own temptations to suicide for unrequited love, so the youthful Jung was able to work through some of his own schizoid splits in writing his dissertation and other works on the psychology of schizoid processes.

For Jung, Helene Preiswerk became the first example he encountered of what he called the law of *enantiodromia*, polar reversal. She went from one pole, her general weakness and silliness and her willingness to cheat, to the opposite pole where she was expressing the best in herself. Helene smuggled objects into the room under her dress and produced them in the dark as if they had materialized through her power as a medium. She was caught in the act and her dishonesty resulted in a break up of the seances. From this case he generalized another psychological law: in order to advance to a higher state of development we often have to commit some mistake so terrible that it may threaten to ruin our lives. 'Then she was able to live out in reality the character she had developed for herself first in the unconscious' (Jung, 1925, p. 6), i.e., through Ivenes and the other subpersonalities who appeared in the seances. Later on this was to be Jung's own experience as well, as he came to live out the mythic images prefigured in his dreams and fantasies. Thus, from the beginning of his psychiatric career, Jung's approach to dream images was teleological and future- rather than past-oriented.

In 1900 Carl Jung moved from Basel to Zurich in order to begin his career as a psychiatrist, working under the guidance of his chief and mentor, Eugene Bleuler at the Burgholzli Mental Hospital. He was glad to leave Basel, because he wanted to strike out on his own, to establish his independence. He felt that in Basel he was permanently marked as the grandson of the famous scholar-physician Carl Gustav Jung, Sr, on the one hand and of his illustrious grandfather, Samuel Preiswerk, the theologian and dean of Basel Cathedral on the other. He felt stifled by the bourgeois complacency of Basel where he belonged to a definite social milieu. Now that he had completed his university medical studies he wanted to make a fresh start in a new environment.

A colleague of Jung's from the Burgholzli described his experience as a young resident in these words:

The patient was the focus of interest. The student learned how to talk with him. Burgholzli was in that time a kind of factory where you worked very hard and were poorly paid. Everyone from the professor to the young resident was totally absorbed by his work. Abstinence from alcoholic drinks was imposed on everyone (Ellenberger, 1970, p. 667).

It must have been hard indeed for young Jung to adapt to this strict regime when he first arrived at the Burgholzli. In Basel as a student he was known as 'the Barrel' for his ability to consume large quantities of beer and wine at his fraternity drinking parties. Suddenly he was cut off from all social life outside the hospital and had little close personal contact with anyone but his patients. In the long run this experience was probably good for him, for it led him to take up the challenge of discovering meaning in what at first appeared to be the nonsensical ravings of lunatics. He became passionately concerned with finding out what actually takes place inside the mentally ill (Jung, 1961, p. 114).

In the light of other accounts of Professor Bleuler and his work at the Burgholzli it seems that in his memoirs Jung exaggerated his uniqueness in being the only one among his colleagues who was really interested in the psychology of the mentally ill.[1] It is understandable that he felt this way, however, and it is probably true that he was more highly motivated in this direction than many of his fellow residents.

Through his own original research and clinical work Jung soon established himself as one of the brightest and most gifted young psychiatrists in Europe. Whereas in Basel he felt burdened by the shadows of his ancestors, here in Zurich he was able to make a name for himself through his own hard work and thereby to tackle the major developmental tasks of early adulthood.

One of his former students, Ludwig Binswanger, offers the following description of Jung at the Burgholzli, circa 1907.

It was C. G. Jung, then chief physician of the hospital, under whom I planned to write my doctor's thesis, who

turned out to be the greatest inspiration of those days.
He kept his students spellbound by his temperament and
the wealth of his ideas. . . . Jung suggested as a subject
for my thesis 'The Psychic-Galvanic Reflex Phenomena in
the Association Test,' a subject that not only proved to
be more and more fascinating the deeper I went into it
but one that brought me into particularly close contact
with Jung. Indeed, he was constantly helping me by
giving me the benefit of his advice and his knowledge
and even by letting me use him as a subject in experiments (Binswanger, 1957, p. 1).

Although Jung admired and learned a great deal from
Professor Bleuler, early on in the relationship he knew he
needed something more, and he was open to finding another
mentor. During the winter of 1902/3 Jung took a leave of
absence from the Burgholzli in order to study under Pierre
Janet in Paris. Janet had become the Professor of Experimental Psychology at the Collège de France. In his lectures
Janet explored the normal and morbid emotions, consciousness, hysteria, and psychotherapy – all subjects which already
fascinated Jung. Janet's views conflicted with those of Freud,
but in the end Jung followed Freud rather than Janet. Jung
enjoyed his stay in Paris and returned to the Burgholzli early
in 1903 full of talk about Janet and his theories (Ellenberger,
1970, p. 668).

Jung was now twenty-eight. He decided it was time to
marry and start a family. He had picked his bride-to-be some
time before, when he was a student, but she had rejected him
because of his poverty. Emma Rauschenbach was the daughter
of a wealthy Schaffhausen industrialist. When he approached
her again, now that he was a successful young physician
she accepted him. They were married on 14 February 1903.
She came from a fine old Swiss-German family and had the
fine education which accompanied her class. She was a good-
looking woman. No one could deny her attractiveness or her
wealth.

Jung's financial troubles were now at an end and his lifestyle changed. Now he could have meals cooked to his taste

rather than institutional food, new clothes, and a big three-room flat instead of a monastic cell at the Burgholzli. The years of his early married life were successful and happy. Children followed each other in succession in two-year intervals. Jung was lucky. Having a stable home life and a dedicated wife, he could pursue his career.

While the years 1903–4 dramatically changed Jung's personal life, they also brought profound changes in his professional development. He seemed headed for a brilliant university career as an academic psychiatrist. In 1904 he was appointed First Oberarzt at the Burgholzli – roughly equivalent to Clinical Director – and became in effect Deputy Director of the entire Burgholzli Mental Hospital. Within a few months he also took over direction of the outpatients department and was granted the coveted title of Privat Dozent (Lecturer) in Psychiatry at the University of Zurich. In the same year he became Senior Physician at the Psychiatric Clinic.

Jung and Freud

For some time Jung had been growing ever more interested in the thinking of Freud. He had read *The Interpretation of Dreams* in 1900 when it was first published, but it was only when he re-read it in 1903 that he realized its importance. By the time he came to write his pioneering analysis of *The Psychology of Dementia Praecox* (schizophrenia) in 1906, he had become thoroughly conversant with Freudian theory and had formed a small informal Freud discussion group that met in his apartment in the Burgholzli (Jung, 1961, p. 146).

Jung was tempted to write to Freud and to visit him in Vienna, but he hesitated. His Freudian activities were already causing him some friction with his mentor, Bleuler, who did not understand or accept the Freudian theory of infantile sexuality. Furthermore, academic life strongly attracted Jung and, at this time, Freud was definitely a *persona non grata* in the academic world. Jung did not want to threaten his own academic career and any connection with Freud could damage rather than enhance his lifework chances. Important people mentioned Freud surreptitiously, but Jung felt it would be risky to cite Freud as an authority in his publications. His discovery that Freud's theories corroborated his own association experiments at the Burgholzli, Jung viewed with mixed feelings. Uncertain whether to mention Freud when he first published his findings in 1906, Jung suddenly heard the Devil whispering to him that such an acknowledgment was unnecessary: 'After all I had worked out my experiment long before I understood his work.' His second personality then intervened to protest and warn him: 'You cannot build your life upon a lie.'[2] Jung now decided openly to sympathize with Freud and his findings (Jung, 1961, p. 148).

Jung initiated the relationship in 1906 by sending Freud a copy of his 'Diagnostic association studies' (1973a), originally published in 1904, a report of some experiments he had conducted with his students which seemed to support the Freudian theory. The two men then struck up a regular correspondence that lasted practically until the outbreak of war in 1914. For months Jung had been filled with eager anticipation at the prospect of his first encounter with the master. Ernest Jones gave the following account of this meeting:

> He [Jung] had very much to tell Freud and to ask him, and with intense animation he poured forth in a spate for three whole hours. The patient, absorbed listener interrupted him with the suggestion that they conduct their discussion more systematically. To Jung's astonishment, Freud proceeded to group the contents of the harangue under several precise headings that enabled him to spend the further hours in a more profitable give and take (Jones, 1955, p. 36).

The description of their respective different styles of behavior already points to some of the irreconcilable differences that were to doom their relationship from the start.

Personal as well as professional factors destined this mentor/apprentice relationship for eventual disaster. Jung himself later attempted to ascribe their final break to differences in personality types. Sociological and political factors also played an important role in drawing these two men together and in pulling them in opposite directions later.

At the start Freud was both very positively attracted towards Jung's personality and grateful for the support Jung brought from abroad. Freud needed external allies in his struggle to crack the Austro-Hungarian academic establishment, for his Austrian followers were disreputable locally and carried little weight in academic circles. Jung also stood to benefit from such an external alliance. Though he looked up to Professor Bleuler, his mentor and chief at the Burgholzli Mental Hospital, his professional life chances in Zurich, as Professor Bleuler's assistant, were quite limited. The Professor was still relatively young; the most that Jung could hope for under his patronage was to become chief assistant, which he had already achieved in 1905. The best way to advance his career more rapidly was to find an ally outside the Swiss school. Having an independent base in Zurich Jung could be an *ally* to Freud, not merely a *disciple*, like the Viennese members of Freud's circle. This relationship was important for both men, coming as it did at a crucial time in their professional careers.

In the Freud-Jung relationship, personal neurotic needs were intermingled with purely professional considerations.[3] Jung soon recognized the 'peculiarity' of his attitude to his mentor:

> My veneration for you has something of the character of
> a religious crush. Though it does not really bother me,
> I still feel it is disgusting and ridiculous because of its
> undeniable erotic undertone. This abominable feeling
> comes from the fact that as a boy I was once the victim
> of a sexual assault by a man I once worshipped (McGuire,
> 1974).

In the early days of their relationship, out of deference to Freud, Jung suppressed his doubts and submitted to Freud's authority thereby stifling his own creative development. When the two men met in 1906 Jung was only thirty-two. He had not yet found his own voice nor developed his own approach. Perhaps his very deference towards his mentor built up a store of repressed energy inside him that finally burst out in his writing of *Symbols of Transformation* in 1912 (1967a), the work in which he first clearly articulated his fundamental theoretical differences from Freud.

As is inevitable when a relationship is based on so many projections, hiding essential and irreconcilable differences, the day of awakening was bound to come, and with it disillusionment, resentment, and bitterness. The emerging rift between Jung and Freud was prefigured, Jung felt, in a dream he had while traveling with Freud to the United States in 1909. To Freud the dream indicated Jung's suppressed wish to destroy and replace him. To Jung the dream 'postulated something of an altogether impersonal nature' 'a first inkling of a collective *a priori* beneath the personal psyche'. (Jung, 1961, p. 160). Their respective differing approaches to dream interpretation became evident in their very different interpretations of this dream. Freud interpreted the dream as pointing backwards, towards repressed infantile wishes; Jung interpreted it as pointing forward, a guiding image prefiguring his own future direction of development.

> This was the dream. I was in a house I did not know, which had two stories. It was 'my house.' I found myself in the upper story, where there was a kind of salon furnished with fine old pieces in rococo style. On the walls hung a number of precious old paintings. I wondered that this should be my house and thought 'Not bad.' But then it occurred to me that I did not know what the lower floor looked like. Descending the stairs, I reached the ground floor. There everything was much older, and I realized that this part of the house must date back to

the fifteenth or sixteenth century. The furnishings were
medieval. The floors were of red brick. Everywhere it was
rather dark. I went from one room to another thinking
'Now I really must explore the whole house.' I came upon
a heavy door and opened it. Beyond it, I discovered a stone
stairway that led down into the cellar. Descending again
I found myself in a beautifully vaulted room which looked
exceedingly ancient. Examining the walls I discovered
layers of brick among the ordinary stone blocks and chips
of brick in the mortar. As soon as I saw this I knew that
the walls dated from Roman times. My interest, by now
was intense. I looked more closely at the floor. It was of
stone slabs and in one of these I discovered a ring. When
I pulled it the stone slab lifted and again I saw a stairway
of narrow steps leading down into the depths. These, too
I descended, and entered a low cave cut into the rock.
Thick dust lay on the floor, and in the dust were scattered
bones and broken potterylike remains of a primitive culture. I discovered two human skulls, obviously very old
and half disintegrated. Then I spoke (Jung, 1961, p. 159).

This dream also revived Jung's earlier youthful interest in
archeology. The part of him that he had suppressed in order
to pursue his practical medical scientific career re-emerged.
He now turned to books on excavations and to studies of
ancient mythology and symbolism.

I read like mad and worked with feverish interest through
a mountain of mythological material, then through the
Gnostic writers, and ended in total confusion. . . . It was as
if I was in an imaginary madhouse and was beginning to
treat and analyze all the centaurs, nymphs, gods, and
goddesses . . . as though they were my patients (Jung,
1961, p. 162).

Mythology now became for him a kind of psychology, a
psychopathology writ large. Through this imaginative leap he
was able to link gods with diseases and so was able to devise
an archetypal basis for the therapy of psychic suffering.

During this period Jung came to see how different his intellectual roots were from Freud's. He had grown up in Basel in a deeply history-conscious milieu, in the atmosphere of Bachofen, Nietzsche, and Burckhardt. Jung loved classical antiquity and the Renaissance. He admired the culture of the seventeenth and eighteenth centuries. As a boy he had imagined himself as a gentleman of that elegant Age of Reason. As a student he had read and enjoyed the great old philosophers and religious thinkers from Plato and Augustine to Kant and Schopenhauer. He had also acquired a knowledge of the history of psychology, especially as presented in the writings of the philosophers.

Furthermore, Jung was an intuitive thinker, temperamentally a nature mystic. His personal experience and childhood in the country had convinced him that:

> Being a part, man cannot grasp the whole. He is at its
> mercy. He may assent to it, or rebel against it; but he
> is always caught up by it. Love is his light and his dark-
> ness, whose end he cannot see. Man can try to name love,
> showering upon it all the names at his command, and
> still he will involve himself in endless self-deceptions.
> If he possess a grain of wisdom, he will lay down his
> arms and name the unknown by the more unknown,
> *ignotum per ignotius* – that is, by the name of God.
> That is a confession of his subjection, his imperfection,
> and his dependence; but at the same time a testimony
> to his freedom to choose between truth and error (Jung,
> 1961, p. 354).

Freud called this worldview infantile. Jung felt it to be the deepest wisdom of maturity and an honest recognition of the limits of human reason *vis-à-vis* the supra-rational, transpersonal, depth dimension in man.

Jung interpreted his dream as being an indication of his unique cultural heritage. It recalled to him his lost self, his suppressed second personality, which the mentorship was limiting. And it pointed to the primitive man within his own heart, a world that could scarcely be reached by consciousness. Jung felt that the salon referred to his ego or conscious mind. But the dream pointed to deeper levels beyond the eighteenth-century rational mind. The floors of the house including the Roman cellar and the prehistoric cave signified past times and passed stages in the history of consciousness, pointing back into prehistory to the origins of consciousness. 'My dream thus constituted a kind of structural diagram of the human psyche; it postulated something of an altogether *impersonal* nature underlying that psyche' (Jung, 1961, p. 161). This dream became for Jung a guiding image in the months ahead as he worked his way through the volumes of mythology attempting to recover his own lost heritage, the history of human consciousness written indelibly in the soul of Everyman.

By the time he wrote *Symbols of Transformation* (1967a), at the age of thirty-six, Jung had made the hero's journey symbolically. He had broken free of the ties with mother. He had gone out into the world, had challenged the leading knights (peers) of the scientific community and the learned world and he had won his spurs. He had become a man. No longer the dumb young Parsifal was he. As a youth he had stood by feeling helpless watching his father die (Jung, 1961, p. 215). He did not know what to say to his father, did not even know what to ask. Later he was to learn the significance of Parsifal's question 'Whom does the Grail serve?' and the answer 'It serves the Grail King.' He came to realize that the Grail King is the Self, that center of our interior castle, that circle whose center is everywhere and whose circumference is nowhere.

In *Symbols of Transformation*, Jung analyzed the normal process of early adult development through the study of a case of a pre-psychotic young woman. Jung does not make a great deal of the fact that she is a woman, but his analysis is a study of adult development of a woman in Western culture. What are the life tasks of this phase of life (young or early adulthood)? Breaking free of one's parents, getting out on one's own, becoming autonomous, self-supporting, self-reliant. Freud summed it up with the words 'love and work.' The tasks of adult life include making peace with one's past, particularly with one's parents; letting go of childhood illusions and infantile attachments and dependency needs, forgiving one's parents, accepting them as limited fallible human beings like oneself, burdened, crippled by the same patterns of negative love that have ruined one's own life; development of flexibility rather than rigidity; development of skills of mastery and competence in areas recognized as valid for a man or woman in one's own culture.

Is it possible that Jung wrote *Symbols of Transformation* when he did, aged thirty-six, as an expression of his growing awareness that he himself was beginning to undergo the transformation of mid-life, marking the entry into a new and different life structure?

For his youth Jung had a myth of initiation – or at least one was readily available if he believed in it. As a Christian he had been baptized and later was confirmed and was allowed to eat and drink from the Lord's Table. However, he found to his chagrin that the Eucharist and the experience of confirmation had little meaning to him (Jung, 1961, p. 75). He experienced them as empty rituals and felt them to be meaningless.

Now Jung faced a new life phase, a new transition for which he had no cultural myth at the ready. Jung indicated this when he wrote 'I had no myth available' after he had completed writing an analysis of the myth governing the development of a young woman. He then decided to take the plunge into the internal underground of the unconscious, to search out his own myth and make the hero's journey that he had written about before.[4]

Now Jung cast aside his former professorial role and humbly submitted himself as a student to the figures of his own unconscious. He learned to understand the language and the meaning of old myths and stories that had educated and entertained the human race long before he was born. Jung learned a deeper meaning for the lore of the tribe which he had first encountered at the literal level when younger.

It is appropriate to consider here the significance of the mentor relationship not only in Jung's life but in adult development more generally. A mentor acts as a teacher to enhance a young man's skills and intellectual development. He may also serve as a sponsor and use his influence to facilitate his protégé's advancement. He may serve as a host or guide, welcoming the intiate into a new occupational and social world, acquainting him with its values, customs, resources, and significant leaders. Through his virtues and achievements the mentor may be an exemplar that the protégé can admire and seek to emulate. He may provide counsel and moral support in time of stress.

The mentor is not a parent or parent surrogate. His primary function is to serve as a transitional figure. In early adulthood a young man must shift from being a child in relation to parental adults to being an adult in a peer relation with other adults. The mentor represents a mixture of parent and peer, though he can be neither. If he is entirely a peer he cannot represent the advanced level toward which the younger man is striving. If he is very parental, it becomes difficult for both men to overcome their generational differences and move toward a peer relationship which is the ultimate goal. Sometimes parents can serve mentoring functions, but they are too closely tied to their offspring's pre-adult development to really serve as mentors.

A mentor is usually ten to fifteen years older than his protégé. Freud was eighteen years older than Jung, almost a full generation older. Freud tended to treat Jung as his 'adopted son and heir.' Jung tended to treat Freud as a father figure. This led to Oedipal conflicts that interfered with the mentoring role. Throughout the correspondence one senses Jung's growing resistance to Freud's paternal demands. The mentoring relationship lasted about six years (from 1906–12). Neither Freud nor Jung seem to have borne in mind Jung's psychological law that a creative person must, ultimately, serve his own creative daimon. In the end the protégé is bound to break with anyone or anything that stands in the way of his realization of his own creativity.

Even though both men were determined to illuminate the dark background of the unconscious, their worldviews were so fundamentally different that a lasting agreement between them was impossible. Freud's background was urban, intellectual, Jewish, and positivistic. His idealized reference was to the British empiricist and utilitarian tradition. He was a rationalist, dedicated to replacing the irrationalities of myth, religion, and the occult sciences with the hard-nosed scientific rationalism and empiricism that characterized the natural sciences in the late nineteenth century. 'Where ID was there Ego shall be,' was Freud's motto. His concern with understanding the unconscious seems to have been motivated by his wish to control and dominate it, a typical Western male attitude, especially in his bourgeois Viennese milieu.

Jung was, in many ways, the antithesis of Freud. His background was rural, religious, and mystical. He grew up in a Protestant pietistic religious milieu which nurtured his own natural penchant for occult and mystical experiences and altered states of consciousness. His immediate philosophical and intellectual roots were nineteenth-century German romantic idealism and *Naturphilosophie*, and beyond that the Platonic and neo-Platonic tradition blended with strong infusions of German mysticism, of Meister Eckhart, Jacob Boehme, Angeles Silesius, and German rationalist philosophers such as Leibniz and Kant. Like Freud, Jung was inspired by the writings of Schopenhauer, Darwin, and Nietzsche, but he drew different conclusions from their works.

Even in the natural sciences their values, attitudes, and reference groups were fundamentally different. For example, Freud was steeped in classical physics. Jung, on the other hand, was interested in the 'new' physics of Einstein, Planck, and Pauli, with whom he had close personal contact. Rejecting the crude oversimplifications of Ernst Heckel and Emile Dubois-Reymond, nineteenth-century positivists whom Freud admired, Jung believed that 'sooner or later nuclear physics and the psychology of the unconscious will draw closer together.'

Their differences in ethnic, religious, philosophical, and scientific backgrounds were also reflected in their opposite personality types. It was, in fact, Jung's attempt to account for the dissolution of this mentor/disciple relationship that led him to develop his theory of psychological types. Jung realized that he was an introvert rather than an extravert, like Freud, in his primary attitude and orientation. For the introvert, subjectivity is the prime motivating factor and objects outside the self are of secondary importance or concern.

Jung found himself by nature and experience fascinated with the secrets of the personality and the phenomenology of his own subjectivity. Freud criticized Jung's attitude as morbid and narcissistic, and his essay 'On narcissism: an introduction' (1917), originally published in 1914, was his response to Jung's 'betrayal.' Whereas Freud emphasized ego mastery over the unconscious, Jung relativized the ego, as one functional complex among others in the psyche, which he viewed as a dynamic self-regulating system. Jung came to approach the unconscious with an attitude of receptivity and almost reverence, as the Great Mother, and source of his vitality, creativity, passion, and delight. To indicate their mutual complementarity one might say that Freud's orientation to the unconscious was very Yang, assertive and controlling, Jung's orientation to the unconscious was more receptive and flowing. His motto was 'Don't interfere; go with the flow.'

Looking back from 1912, we see that Jung had come a long way in his development during these years. In 1900 when he joined the staff of the Burgholzli, he was a burgeoning young physician with his future before him. In the ensuing years he married and had a family and established himself in his chosen career as a psychiatrist. He won worldly acclaim early for his original research and work with the association experiment at the Burgholzli and for his analysis of schizophrenia. He met and befriended Freud, becoming his right-hand man and heir apparent. He suffered the dilemmas of discipleship and eventually made the decision to strike out on his own in 1912. This decision cost him his friendship with Freud and as a consequence he lost most of his other friends and associates in the psychoanalytic movement. But he had himself, and in the exploration of his own dreams and fantasies in the years ahead he was to discover and articulate his own psychotherapeutic vision and his own myth.

In this chapter we have traced Jung's early adult development. During the years 1900–12 Jung accomplished the developmental tasks of early adulthood, establishing a home, a family, and beginning a successful ascent up the career ladder as a scholar and physician in a Swiss mental hospital. He could have settled for the security of that position, but instead he felt the need to break out of this safe environment. The alliance he developed with Freud offered him a pathway to worldly power and success beyond what he could ever hope for if he remained within the conservative assumptive world of Dr Bleuler and Swiss psychiatry. For a time Jung managed to maintain an uneasy balance between these two rival scientific/therapeutic systems, but eventually he had to choose between these two mentors, Bleuler and Freud. In the end he rejected both of them and developed his own alternative therapeutic system.

Chapter 3
Jung's mid-life transition

This chapter focuses on Jung's mid-life crises, and his personal and intellectual development during the years 1912 to 1922. After his break with Freud and the international psychoanalytic movement, Jung felt intellectually and spiritually alone. In his isolation he turned neither to a new group, such as an organized political, religious or scientific movement, nor to refuge in the security of conventional activities relating to his work and family life. Instead, he turned within to explore the personified images of his interior vision. During this painfully difficult life transition all of his former accomplishments, his values and lifelong commitments were thrown into question. All but overcome by violent feelings and images that he recognized as borderline psychotic, Jung undertook his own self-analysis paralleling Freud's mid-life self-analysis fifteen years earlier. In his desperation Jung found a place to go that was no longer Vienna, figures to communicate with who were no longer the psychoanalytic circle of colleagues, and a father figure and counsellor who was no longer Freud. This encounter with these personal figures initiated Jung into his post-mid-life path, the healing journey of individuation. They became the personification of his calling which combined religion and medicine in the cure of souls, or soul-making (Hillman, 1975).

During the First World War Jung experienced his own inner world war and revolution. He went through a process of breakdown and transformation that we have since come to know, partly through his writings, as the mid-life transition.

In his memoirs Jung exaggerated his isolation and his heroism in confronting the forces and figures that threatened him from within. While we cannot but admire his courage and creativity in facing his inner turmoil, it should be recognized that throughout this period he had the emotional and financial support of his wife, Emma Jung, as well as of his lovers and friends. Not everyone can afford the experience of a mid-life breakdown. Most people are too preoccupied with meeting their basic survival needs. The Jungian way is not for everybody; it is designed for a creative elite.

Jung made the most of his opportunity for self-analysis, and acknowledged that one must pay one's dues to society and purchase the right to individuation. He felt it was his duty to learn from his experience and translate his newly acquired insight into a contribution to the science of psychology.

In his memoirs Jung acknowledged that the dream/vision quest he made during these years laid the foundation for his further intellectual development. As he put it:

> The years when I was pursuing my inner images were the most important in my life – in them everything essential was decided. It all began then. The later details are only supplements and clarifications of the material that burst forth from the unconscious, and at first swamped me. It was the *prima materia* for a lifetime's work . . . . It has taken me virtually forty-five years to distill within the vessel of my scientific work the things I experienced and wrote down at that time. As a young man my goal had been to accomplish something in my science. But then I hit upon this stream of lava, and the heat of its fire reshaped my life (Jung, 1961, p. 199).

I find this quotation fascinating because it indicates in a few words the essence of Jung's mid-life transition. In early adulthood he had sought 'to accomplish something in [his] science,' and he did accomplish those ego goals by the time he reached his late thirties. The break with Freud, the World War, marital difficulties, and other psychic and social factors combined to throw Jung into a profound questioning of everything he had been and believed in up to this point in his life. It was necessary to clear the decks to make a space for the emergence of a new life structure. Only after he gave in, gave up the defensive life structure created by the first personality and allowed himself to experience his own inner darkness, what he called his shadow, was Jung ready to open himself to experience the 'stream of lava and the heat of its fire' which reshaped his life. But once he experienced it, he felt compelled to work upon it, and viewed his works as 'a more or less successful endeavour to incorporate this incandescent matter into the contemporary world picture' (ibid., p. 199).

What were the issues Jung faced as he approached mid-life and how did he resolve them? he had to go through the painful dissolution of his old life structure and to experience his feelings of guilt, loss, loneliness, isolation, and even failure. He had to face the painful fact of his own aging process and the inevitability of his eventual death. He had to face and integrate some of the non-ego aspects of himself and work through some of the basic polarities in the psyche. Out of this mid-life passage Jung discovered the Self as a new integrating center of the personality beyond the ego.

In his essay on 'The ego and the unconscious' written in 1928, Jung differentiated his concept of the Self from the 'ego.' For Jung the Self is 'supraordinate to the conscious ego' (Jung, 1966a, p. 177). It embraces both the conscious and the unconscious psyche. In his usage the ego 'is only the center of my field of consciousness and is not identical with the totality of my psyche' (Jung, 1971, p. 425). He distinguished between ego and Self since 'the ego is only the subject of my consciousness while the Self is the subject of my total psyche which also includes the unconscious' (Jung, 1971, p. 425). In this sense the Self is an 'ideal entity which embraces the ego.' The Self is our life's goal for it is the completest expression of that fateful combination we call individuality' (Jung, 1966a, p. 240). In Jung's usage the Self refers to both center and totality of the personality; ego-development is subordinated to self-development.

From his own experience Jung concluded that the task of the second half of life was the development of the Self, bringing about a greater wholeness, roundedness and groundedness than could be attained through ego-development alone. In the second half of life, Jung found we need to develop those aspects of ourselves that remained underdeveloped in our early adulthood. Self-development results from the dialectical interplay of ego and non-ego, or conscious and unconsious, aspects of the personality. One must not give up ego entirely, Jung warned, for therein lies psychosis. The task is to develop a balanced relationship between ego and Self, in order to grow towards greater wholeness (Jung, 1966a).

Now let us examine Jung's personal experience of his own mid-life transition for this will help us to understand and to contextualize his theory of the individuation process in the second half of life.

In 1911 as he approached mid-life the prospects for the future appeared very positive to Carl Jung. He seemed to be successful. He felt that he had achieved the objectives he had aspired to in early adulthood. He had a stable happy marriage and family, a flourishing private practice as a psychiatrist, and he was the acknowledged heir-apparent to Freud, and the President of the International Psychoanalytic Association. He had no idea that in the years ahead war was on the horizon nor that he was to be all but overcome in a struggle with his own inner demons. Within the next few years Jung was to see his early adult life structure crumble and fall apart before his eyes.

Jung's mid-life crisis has been variously interpreted as everything from a heroic conquest of the unconscious to a psychotic breakdown (Brome, 1978; Ellenberger, 1970; Storr, 1974; Stern, 1976; Van der Post, 1975; Von Franz, 1975). From his memoirs and sympathetic biographers it appears that Jung voluntarily made a conscious decision to confront the imagery of the collective unconscious at mid-life. Perhaps a more objective interpretation is to suggest that what happened to Jung at this time was beyond his control, but his creative manner of coping with his breakdown was a result of his conscious choice and effort. The details of this experience in Jung's life are worth careful examination because Jung believed that his later work derived directly from this experience (Jung, 1961, p. 192).

After the break with Freud, Jung acknowledged that 'a period of inner uncertainty' began for him. This state of 'disorientation' was deeply disturbing to him in many ways. He began to be subject to long periods of depression and despair, to feel that his former scientific work was valueless and that he himself was a misfit. Inner voices battered and persecuted his wounded and vulnerable self-esteem. It seemed to him that all his friends had deserted him. He admitted feeling literally as if he were suspended in mid-air and had, so to speak, lost his footing (ibid., p. 170).

In 1912 he had completed a major work on the psychology of mythology, *Symbols of Transformation* (2nd edn, 1967a), but he did not feel happy about the book despite the impact it made in psychological circles and the revolutionary ideas he had proposed in it. 'It was written at top speed amid the rush and press of my medical practice without regard to time and method.' He had flung the material together as it poured out of him 'like a landslide' which could not be stopped. He felt that 'it was the explosion of all those psychic contents which could find no . . . breaking space in the constricting atmosphere of Freudian psychology' (Jung, 1967a, p. xxiii). The driven compulsive quality of his writing might have indicated to him that deeper forces were stirring within him. When he finished the work he felt empty and lost, facing a void within and without. He began to have unsettling dreams of cosmic conflagrations, of erupting volcanoes, of terrifying dark figures that pursued him, and of corpses which came back to life. With his waking consciousness he had organized and mastered the strange world of mythology, but at night these designs of the underworld broke out of the pages of his book to haunt and taunt him.

Now that he had analyzed the psychology of mythology he began to ask himself the more personal question – by what myth do I live? He concluded with Nietzsche that his God was dead, that the myth of the Jewish–Christian God no longer guided his thought and action. He found the mythology of the Greco-Roman world fascinating as an intellectual exercise, but it was not his myth either. His close scrutiny of possible answers left him so baffled and uncomfortable that at last he decided to abandon the quest.

Internal conflicts now became so intense that he found he could no longer lecture coherently and he abandoned his academic career by withdrawing from his position as a Privat Dozent (Lecturer) at the University of Zurich after eight continuous years. This psychologically enforced abdication of his role as a university teacher was very painful to Jung. He later told Anthony Storr that 'he knew what sacrifice meant because of this abandonment of an academic career' (Storr, 1974). These inner conflicts also led him to reduce his private practice to a minimum. He became more and more preoccupied with his own inner life.

As if these inner pressures were not enough, on top of everything else, Jung's marriage and family now became seriously threatened as a result of Jung's marital infidelities. Jung wrote 'the pre-requisite for a good marriage, it seems to me, is the license to be unfaithful' (McGuire, 1974, p. 289). His wife did not agree. Tall and handsome as he was, Jung was always surrounded by a number of women whose interests in him and his work were often more than purely scientific. During the years 1911 to 1912 Jung fell in love with one of his patients, Antonia Wolff, then aged twenty-three. Their relationship slowly escaped its professional restraints and produced complicated repercussions on Jung's family life. One of the other women in his circle of admirers grew very jealous and revealed to Emma that her husband was sleeping with Antonia. According to Paul J. Stern in his *C. G. Jung: The Haunted Prophet*, 'Jung's affair with Toni might have been less troublesome if he had not insisted on drawing his mistress into his family life and on having her as a regular guest for Sunday dinner' (Stern, 1976, p. 138). As his relationship with Toni Wolff developed, Emma found the situation increasingly difficult but Jung firmly opposed dissolution of their marriage. He needed Emma. He told her that he loved her and wanted to preserve the family. He could not help it if he had fallen in love with another woman as well. Emma would always be his wife. Toni was his soul sister, his *soror mysticas*. Emma must have felt moved by love and perhaps by pity for Carl Jung for she agreed to stay with him and remained his solid support during the difficult time of his mid-life transition. Somehow Jung managed to convince both his wife and his mistress that he needed both of them, and for his sake they should stay on friendly terms. Though there was a good deal of strain in these relationships for a time, eventually the three worked out an amicable arrangement.

Turning to another woman, usually younger than one's wife, is a classic pattern of behavior of men at mid-life. The younger woman, who does not bear the burden of domestic chores, wifely duties, such as budget management or bringing up the children, can give a middle-aged man the feeling of new youth and freedom. Sometimes she can act as an inspiration to him, encouraging him to strike out in new directions. Often these mid-life affairs are short-lived. Sometimes they lead to divorce and re-marriage. In Jung's case the relationship with Antonia Wolff lasted for over fifty years, but after the initial shock of recognition Toni ceased to be a threat to Jung's marital life and became integrated into the family rather like an old maid aunt.

Early in the year 1913 he set out for a four-day cruise on Lake Zurich with Albert Oeri and several other younger friends. During the voyage Oeri read aloud the Nekyia episode from Homer's *Odyssey*, the journey of Ulysses to the realm of the dead. Jung was now approaching what he considered to be the most shattering experience of his life. He later frequently referred to it as his own Nekyia. His dreams returned again and again to the theme of death and of corpses that were not really dead.

'One fantasy kept returning: there was something dead present, but it was also still alive. For example, corpses were placed in crematory ovens, but were then discovered to be still living. These fantasies came to a head and were simultaneously resolved in a dream' (Jung, 1961, p. 172). In this dream Jung saw himself walking down a long row of elevated tombs upon which the dead knights lay mummified. Under his intense gaze they became animated, came to life. What was there in his past that would not stay dead and buried? Was this a repressed death wish against his former mentor, as Freudians suggest? Jung interpreted this and other similar dreams as indicating that he must reconcile himself with his own cultural and historical roots. He studied Gnosticism and hermetic alchemy, the dark shadow side of medieval Christianity. He meditated on stories of the Knights of the Holy Grail and their quest – 'for that was, in the deepest sense, my own world, which had scarcely anything to do with Freud's. My whole being was seeking for something still unknown which might confer meaning upon the banality of life' (ibid., p. 165).

Jung's dreams and fantasies were so intense that he soon concluded that there was 'some psychic disturbance' in himself, and he now began his own self-analysis, a process which was to lead him into the deepest and most volcanic regions of his psyche and carry his theories into new and original fields. Whether the initial steps in his self-analysis were deliberately taken or whether, like many other mentally disturbed persons, he regressed involuntarily we do not know. In anyone else the straightforward term 'breakdown' would describe the general characteristics of what took place, but I agree with Brome that 'with a psyche so complex, rich and powerful every conceivable complication cross-fertilised the process until the rationally willed was indistinguishable from the compulsively inescapable' (Brome, 1978, p. 158).

Jung now went very carefully over all the details of his early life paying special attention to his early childhood memories. The first recollection thrown up by the past revealed Jung as a child playing passionately with building blocks to create an array of castles, temples, and houses. Emotional reactions erupted in this recollection which he felt he could hardly control. He decided that he could only bridge the gap between the adult man of thirty-six and the small boy within him by once more playing childish games

(Jung, 1961, p. 173). This idea seemed so repugnant to him at first that he could not voluntarily submit. The fact that he put up endless resistances and only succumbed with resignation suggests that neurotic compulsions played a major part in driving him back down those painful paths of memory.

Continuously the question recurred – what exactly was he doing and why, and as consistently back came the answer – 'discovering my own myth,' but the building game proved only the beginning of what was to become a whole multitude of self-revealing fantasies. Slowly the stream mounted until 'I stood helplesss before an alien world' and the inner tensions multiplied. There came a time when he felt as if 'gigantic blocks of stone were tumbling down upon him' and one colossal thunderstorm followed on the heels of the last 'My enduring these storms was a question of brute strength,' he wrote, but a driving purpose to discover what it all meant also contributed to his survival. While he 'endured these assaults of the unconscious' he had 'an answering conviction' that he was 'obeying a higher will' (ibid., p. 177).

He now found himself so wrought up that he had to do Hatha Yoga exercises to hold his emotions in check. In the late summer of 1913 he decided to resist any further withdrawal into himself for a while and he began to feel the pressures moving outwards into external life again. He knew very well the danger and terrifying possibilities of becoming completely split off from reality, but now he sought to return to that reality 'the atmosphere actually seemed to me darker than it had been before.' He became convinced that the 'oppression no longer came from an inner psychic situation but from external reality' (ibid., p. 175).

In the autumn of 1913, when traveling alone on some unspecified journey, Jung began to imagine that the railway track was invaded by a great flood of water which slowly overwhelmed the lowlands between the North Sea and the Alps and roared on to threaten Switzerland itself, but as the tide ran across the outer boundaries the mountains seemed to climb higher and higher into the sky as if to escape the flood. Jung saw mighty yellow waves, the floating rubble of civilization, and thousands of drowned bodies. Then the whole sea turned into blood. This vision lasted for over an hour and left him nauseated and exhausted. A few weeks later this vision was repeated and an inner voice spoke to him saying, 'Look at it well; it is wholly real and it will be so. You cannot doubt it' (ibid., p. 175). Soon afterwards when a friend asked Jung what he thought about the future of Europe he admitted that he saw 'rivers of blood.' At the time, however, he did not really imagine that these fantasies pointed toward a European or world war. He took them personally to mean that he himself was menaced by a psychosis (ibid., p. 176).

Not long afterward Jung had another vision. This time it was an Arctic cold wave that was sweeping across the wasteland of Europe. All living green things were killed by frost. The vision repeated itself in April, May, and again in June 1914. This last time there stood a leaf-bearing tree, but without any fruit – 'my tree of life,' he thought – whose leaves had been transformed by the effects of the frost into sweet grapes full of healing juices. He plucked the grapes and gave them to a large waiting crowd (ibid., p. 176). Perhaps this dream gave Jung a sign of his mission as he later conceived it to be, for he came to see himself as being like Parsifal (ibid., p. 215), faced with the task of bringing new life to the dying culture of Western Christendom in the wake of the death of God. The 'sweet grapes full of healing juices' were the images from the unconscious he had learned to interpret.

Jung found that 'to the extent that I managed to translate the emotions into images – that is to find the images concealed in the emotions – I was inwardly calmed and reassured' (ibid., p. 177). He felt that if he had not deciphered their secrets he might have been torn to pieces by them. From his experience he learned how helpful it can be to find the particular images which lie behind our emotions and to work with these images in a creative way. He found that the unconscious tends to speak in a high-flown language, even bombastically. Even though it repelled him, he indulged in this high rhetoric. 'I had no choice but to write everything down in the style selected by the unconscious itself' (ibid., p. 178). Below the threshold of consciousness he felt 'everything was seething with life.' His tree of life, which had been dead for so long, was now burgeoning forth with new fruits. Though the products appeared first in strange quaint forms, Jung later reworked them into the core concepts of his own analytical psychology.

Sometimes Jung felt so terrified by his oscillating moods and strange and painful visionary experiences that he was tempted to call a halt to the whole process. What kept him going, he says was the idea that 'I was committing myself to a dangerous enterprise not for myself alone, but also for the sake of my patients' (ibid., p. 179). He was afraid of losing control, but he decided that there was no way out. He felt that he had to gain power over these fantasies or else they would engulf him. He also felt that he must go through with this 'scientific experiment' because 'I could not expect something of my patients that I would not dare to do myself' (ibid., p. 178).

In December 1913 he resolved to take the decisive step and to give himself over unreservedly to experiencing his fantasies. By this time he had begun to develop some techniques for working with the images that came to him and some techniques for centering himself when he felt he might be overwhelmed. He was sitting at his desk, thinking over his fears, when the image of a giant abyss appeared before him. He decided to let himself drop. He felt the ground give way beneath him and he plunged into dark depths. Then, abruptly, he landed on his feet in a soft, sticky mass. It was dark, but his eyes grew accustomed to the gloom and he saw before him the entrance to a cave in which stood a dwarf with leathery skin, as if he were mummified. Jung waded past the dwarf to the other side of the cave where on a projecting rock he saw a glowing red crystal. He lifted it up and discovered a hollow underneath filled with running water, in which floated a corpse, a youth with blond hair and a wound in the head. He was followed by a gigantic black scarab and then by a red, newborn sun, rising up out of the depths of the water. Jung, dazzled by the light, sought to replace the stone on the opening but then a thick jet of blood leapt up and spurted for a long time. He felt nauseated as the vision ceased (ibid., p. 179).

What was the meaning of these visions of corpses and out-pouring floods of blood? A dream he had a few days later may help us to understand this strange visionary sequence. In this dream Jung was standing beside an unknown brown-skinned man, a savage, in a lonely rocky mountain landscape. It was before dawn. The stars were fading. Then he heard Siegfried's horn sounding over the mountains. He knew that he must kill Siegfried. Armed with rifles, Jung and his dark accomplice lay in wait. When Siegfried appeared on the mountaintop in the first rays of the rising sun they shot him down. Jung felt guilty for destroying something so great and beautiful. He turned to flee, fearing that his crime would be discovered, but rain came and washed all traces of the deed away. Life could go on, but an unbearable sense of guilt remained.

When Jung awoke from the dream he felt unable to under-stand it. He tried to go back to sleep but a voice insisted 'You *must* understand this dream at once. If you do not under-stand it you must shoot yourself' (ibid., p. 180). He had a revolver in the drawer of his night table. He reflected on the dream, and on his revolver and suddenly the meaning of the dream came to him. 'Siegfried represents what the Germans want to achieve, heroically to impose their own will, have their own way. . . . I had wanted to do the same. The dream showed that the attitude embodied by Siegfried, the hero, no longer suited me. Therefore it had to be killed.' He now felt great compassion for Siegfried seeing him as a part of himself that he had been forced to kill. 'My heroic idealism had to be abandoned, for there are higher things than the ego's will, and to these one must bow' (ibid., p. 181). He concluded that the small brown-skinned man who had taken the initiative in the killing was an embodiment of what he called 'the primitive shadow.' The rain showed that the tension between conscious and unconscious was being resolved. Though he did not understand all of the implications of this dream, Jung felt that with these few hints new forces were released inside which enabled him to carry on his experiment with the unconscious to its conclusion.

In order to seize hold of his fantasies Jung practiced imagining himself on a steep descent attempting to get to the bottom. Soon he found himself at the edge of a cosmic abyss. As he let himself drop into this empty space he felt he was in the land of the dead. It had an eerie quality. In the distance he caught sight of two strange figures, an old man with a white beard and a beautiful young girl. He approached and conversed with them. The old man explained that he was Elijah. The girl called herself Salome. She was blind. Jung learned that this pair belonged together for all eternity (ibid., p. 181). The full meaning of these figures only became clear to Jung later. In his memoirs he explained that Salome was an anima figure, an image of his soul. Elijah represented the archetype of the wise old man, embodying Jung's own inner wisdom or knowingness. Eventually Elijah metamorphosed into Philemon, an Egyptian Hellenistic figure. Philemon first appeared to Jung in the following dream:

> There was a blue sky, like the sea, covered not by clouds but by flat brown clods of earth. It looked as if the clods were breaking apart and the blue water of the sea was becoming visible between them. Suddenly there appeared from the right a winged being sailing across the sky. I saw that it was an old man with the horns of a bull. He held a bunch of four keys one of which he clutched as if he were about to open a lock. He had the wings of a kingfisher with its characteristic colors (ibid., p. 182).

Jung was fascinated by the numinous quality of Philemon and proceeded to paint this personification of his unconscious and to carry on extensive dialogues with it. Philemon brought home to Jung the realization that there are things in the psyche which do not produce ourselves, which have their own life (ibid., p. 183). Later Philemon became relativized by the emergence of another figure whom Jung called Ka (ibid., p. 184). In Egypt the Pharoah's Ka was his earthly form, his embodied soul. In Jung's fantasy the Ka-soul came from out of the depths of the earth. He made a painting of Ka, showing him in his earth-bound form as a herm with base of stone. High up in the painting appears a kingfisher's wing. Between it and the head of Ka floats a young, glowing nebula of stars. Ka's expression is almost demonic. In one hand he holds a reliquary, in the other a stylus. Years later through his study of alchemy Jung felt that he arrived at a deeper understanding of these figures, but their function at the time was to serve as the vehicles through which he taught himself what he needed to know in order to move on into the next phase of his life. Salome, the lovely blind girl, was the spokesperson for Jung of his feelings. She was blind, like feelings, because she lacked the insight of knowledge. While Salome represented his feelings, Philemon represented his inner wisdom. Through these experiences with non-ego aspects of himself, Jung began to develop underdeveloped aspects of himself and grew towards greater wholeness.

Jung compared his own Nekyia with Odysseus's visit to the realm of the dead. Here he encountered a fund of unconscious images similar to those shades from Hades. This is not surprising for this fund of unconscious imagery is also the matrix of the mythopoeic imagination. Though this imagination is present in everyone and in cultures all over the world, it is tabooed and dreaded. Yet Jung decided to take the risk and make this journey saying with Goethe's *Faust*: 'Now let me dare to open wide the gate past which men's steps have ever flinching trod' (*Faust*, Part II, Act I).

How did Jung resolve the issues he faced at mid-life? Having broken with Freud and his followers, in 1913 Jung felt a gnawing sense of loss and an emptiness inside. He was also troubled with guilt feelings. He had sacrificed his alliance with his friend and mentor for the sake of following his own vision. In time he was to discover an inner authority and mentor in himself, a figure he called Philemon. But first he went through a period of feeling lost, alone, and guilty. He went into his own void and discovered untold riches there. The symbolic images he encountered in his 'confrontation with the unconscious' provided him with the *prima materia* and the symbolic context for the development of his own system of analytical psychology. It should be emphasized that Jung's experience was not typical. These kinds of very dramatic events are not part of the mid-life transition for most people.

In going through his mid-life transition Jung pursued a direct confrontation with his unconscious, and in the process he re-experienced repressed aspects of his early childhood. He reconnected with the religious traditions he had abandoned while being a Freudian and found nourishment in these religious roots. This symbolic framework allowed him to interpret his visions as religious experience rather than as madness or psychosis as a non-religious psychoanalyst might do.

He had dreams of something dead being still alive or coming back to life. These dreams and visions referred to aspects of himself (his second personality) which he had not included in his early adult life structure, dominated by the first personality.

What is the meaning of all the imagery of death and rebirth, of things being dead yet still alive? I think these images point to Jung's own deep religious roots that were suppressed but still alive within his unconscious. In the course of his mid-life journey, Jung rediscovered his own soul and its religious roots. After this he attempted to lead modern man back to recover his own lost soul. The reversal of libido he experienced in the course of his 'creative illness' activated a great deal of potentially creative imagery. Jung worked with this and used it as a source for his further work. This is one of the principle differences between Jung and a madman who might have experienced similar imagery but done nothing with it.

In 1916 Jung began to feel an impulse to give shape to his new visions. He felt 'compelled from within, as it were, to formulate and express what might have been said by Philemon' (Jung, 1961, p. 190). One day he felt a vague restlessness. He felt the pressure of spirits, but he did not know what 'they' wanted from him. He felt that his house was haunted. Around five o'clock on a Sunday afternoon the front doorbell began to ring furiously. It was a bright summer day. Everyone looked to see who was there, but there was no one in sight.

> I was sitting near the doorbell, and not only heard it, but saw it moving. We all simply stared at one another. The atmosphere was thick, believe me! Then I knew that something had to happen, the whole house was filled as if there were a crowd present, crammed full of spirits. They were packed deep right up to the door, and the air was so thick it was scarcely possible to breathe (ibid., p. 190).

'For God's sake, what in the world is this?' Jung asked himself, feeling nervous and all aquiver. The chorus of spirits now answered him: 'We have come from Jerusalem where we found not what we have sought' (ibid., p. 378).

Out of this experience Jung was prompted to write the *Septem Sermones ad Mortuos* (1967b), which he published under a pseudonym because he felt it was dictated by his daimon. It flowed out of him, as the lines of *Also Sprach Zarathustra* poured out of Nietzsche. In the course of three evenings the whole thing was written. 'As soon as I took up the pen the whole ghostly assemblage evaporated. The room quieted and the atmosphere cleared. The haunting was over' (ibid., p. 191).

Very gradually the outlines of an inner change began making their appearance in Jung. During the remainder of his life, these spirits became ever more distinct. Gradually he came to recognize that the questions and demands they required him to answer did not come from outside but from inside his own psyche. These conversations with the spirits formed a kind of prelude to what he was later to teach to others as the visualization technique he called 'active imagination.' He was like a shaman who, having been given a special vision, translated it into terms meaningful to his tribe. 'It was then that I ceased to belong to myself alone,' he said, 'for there were things in the images which concerned not only myself but many others also. From then on my life belonged to mankind' (ibid., p. 192). To put this differently one might say that as Jung moved from early adulthood to middle adulthood he shifted from the personal to the collective or transpersonal dimension of the psyche and from the ego to the Self as his center and goal.

Jung recognized that the knowledge which was being revealed to him could not be found in the science of the day. 'I myself had to undergo the original experience, and then to try to plant the results of my experience in the soil of reality; otherwise they would have remained subjective assumptions without validity' (ibid.). From this time on he dedicated himself to the service of his daimon, believing that only by delivering himself over to it could he live his life as fully as possible.

Let us consider now how these visualizations, dreams, and fantasies aided Jung in accomplishing the *enantiodromia* (great reversal) of the mid-life transition. Recall that, as he entered mid-life, Jung felt isolated and guilty. He had lost his friend and mentor Freud. In fact he had betrayed him when, as heir apparent to the psychoanalytic throne, he published a work that, from Freud's point of view, was filled with heresy. He was no longer a Freudian. He did not know what to do. His own inner voices showed him the way. He listened to them and translated this esoteric wisdom into a new approach to personal development and psychotherapy. In other words he found that the solution to his problem was to develop his own ideas, and to become the first Jungian.

As he emerged from his mid-life crisis, Jung found solace and psychic integration came to him through painting, stone-carving, and sailing. He felt that these physical and artistic activities balanced him and enabled him to develop his underdeveloped sensation function. In particular, Jung learned a great deal about himself and his own psycho-dynamics by producing a series of circular drawings, called mandalas, which he used as indicators of his daily psychic states.

Although at first Jung could only dimly understand these mandala drawings, he guarded them like precious jewels and kept them in a special leather-bound book which he treasured as part of his own personal sacred scriptures. In time, he felt that he acquired a living conception and representation of the self through these unusual drawings. From these mandalas Jung learned that 'the Self is like a living monad which I am and which is my world' (ibid., p. 196).

When he began his mid-life confrontation with the unconscious Jung had to give up the superordinate position of his ego and let himself be carried along by the flow of his psychic energy without having a clue where he was going. Through his drawing of these mandalas, he felt that he gradually began to see things more clearly. 'All the steps I had taken were leading back to a single point – namely to the mid-point,' Jung later wrote (ibid., p. 197). He began to regard the mandala as a graphic representation of the Self. In fact it was a representation of the totality of the psyche, which Jung regarded as a harmonious self-regulating system, a kind of universe in which the Self is the center about which the ego and other functional complexes, such as the persona (mask), the shadow, and the anima or animus revolve. In Jung's eyes the mandala was like an x-ray of the psyche at a moment in time, a dynamic picture which captured the psychic reality of 'Formation, Transformation, Eternal Mind's eternal recreation' (ibid., p. 196).

In his mandalas Jung believed that he saw the Self – the center of his whole being – actively at work, and he became convinced that drawing and studying one's mandalas offered a way of proceeding to the center of one's being and of allowing the Self to unfold and reveal itself to ego consciousness. Jung concluded from his experience with these mandalas

that 'the goal of psychic development is the Self' (ibid.,
p. 197). He felt that in finding the mandala as an expression
of the Self he had attained the ultimate wisdom he could
attain at that point in his life. In his later life he elaborated
his vision further, but the essence and the goal of the process
of individuation became clear to him at mid-life through his
personal experience and his artistic elaboration of the images
that came to him from the depths of the creative psyche.
Henceforth, there could only be a continual circumambulation of the Self. There is no linear evolution nor progressive
development of the Self, as there is with the ego, because
the Self is there from the beginning. 'Perhaps someone else
knows more, not I,' Jung concluded in his memoirs as he
reflected upon his discovery of the Self through his own
inner psycho-spiritual work.

In 1927 Jung felt that his ideas about the center and the
Self were confirmed by a dream he had. After he awoke he
worked with the dream imagery for some time. As was his
practice when working with dreams and hypnogogic imagery,
he decided to make a painting expressing his feelings about
the dream. The result was a mandala painting he called,
'Window on Eternity.'[1]

A year later Jung painted another mandala, this time with
a golden castle in the center of a fortified city surrounded by
a wall and beyond that a moat and another wall fortified by
sixteen towers. When it was finished Jung looked at it with
surprise. The form and choice of colors seemed 'Chinese' to
him though he had not intended to make a Chinese picture
at all.

Shortly afterwards, Jung received a letter from his friend,
Richard Wilhelm, the translator of the Chinese book of
oracles, the *I Ching*. Along with the letter Wilhelm enclosed
his translation of a Taoist alchemical text, *The Secret of the
Golden Flower*, with a request that Jung write a psychological
commentary on it. Jung was fascinated with the manuscript
because he felt it gave him 'undreamed of confirmation of
my ideas about the mandala and the circumambulation of the
center' (ibid., p. 197). He felt that his receiving this text

soon after he had painted the Chinese-style mandala was more than a coincidence; it was a synchronicity. This event was extremely important to him because he felt that it broke the spell of his seemingly endless isolation. 'I became aware of an affinity; I could establish ties with someone and something' (ibid.).

During his mid-life transition Jung felt very lonely and isolated. It seemed to him that he could tell no one about his disturbing thoughts. He feared that he would be misunderstood and perhaps even locked up as insane. The gulf between his inner world and his social roles seemed enormous and unbridgeable. For many years he felt torn apart by the seemingly irreconcilable conflict of the opposites, inner and outer, which he felt were related to the long-standing conflict between his two personalities (see page 23 above).

Jung became convinced that he could only make contact with the outer world and with people if he could show that the contents of his psychic experience were real and objective. He sought to do this by demonstrating with examples drawn from comparative cultural history and ethnology that his experience corresponded with the collective experience of the human race. It was in part Jung's sense of isolation after his break with Freud that drove him to elaborate his theory of the archetypes of the collective unconscious. It was this same sense of isolation that drove Jung to find historical antecedents to his work. He felt that if he did not succeed in connecting his own experience to the collective experience of mankind he would be forever 'condemned to absolute isolation' (ibid., p. 195).

In the 1920s and 1930s Jung ransacked the history of mankind 'to find evidence for the historical prefiguration of [his] inner experiences' (ibid., p. 200). He asked himself 'Where have my particular premises already occurred in history?' feeling that he needed to find such evidence to substantiate his own ideas. In his search for an historical analogue or reference group, Jung first seized hold of the early Christian Gnostics, finding that 'they too had been confronted with the primal world of the unconscious and had dealt with its contents, with images that were obviously contaminated with the world of instinct.' (ibid., p. 201).

Jung's choice of the Gnostics is very understandable; like him they were fascinated with the conflicts of opposites, and with a kind of dialectical interplay between consciousness and the unconscious, or the ego and the Self, though, of course, they couched their speculative ruminations in more theological terms. In the end, however, the Gnostics seemed too distant, and Jung continued to search for the missing link to his own work.

It was not until 1928 that Jung discovered that alchemy provided the connection he was looking for. He felt that it 'formed the bridge on the one hand into the past, to Gnosticism, and on the other into the future, to the modern psychology of the unconscious' (ibid., p. 201).

Before his discovery of alchemy, Jung had a series of dreams which repeatedly dealt with the same theme. He kept dreaming of a house standing next to his, a house which he did not know. Finally in one dream he entered the house and discovered there a wonderful library dating from the sixteenth and seventeenth centuries. It was much later that he realized that the books contained alchemical symbols. Jung interpreted this house as being an image of a part of his own personality, 'something that belonged to me, but of which I was not yet conscious.' Fifteen years later he assembled a library very similar to the one in the dream.

The crucial dream anticipating his encounter with alchemy came around 1926. He was in the South Tyrol during the First World War. Driving back from the Front with a peasant in a horse-drawn wagon, he saw before him a manor house. They drove in through a gate. As they reached the middle of the courtyard the gates flew shut. The peasant leapt down from his seat and exclaimed 'Now we are caught in the seventeenth century.' Jung felt very frustrated. Then the thought came to him: 'Someday, years from now I shall get out again' (ibid., p. 203). It was several years later that Jung concluded that the dream was message from the unconscious indicating his future interest in alchemy, which reached its height in the seventeenth century.

What was so appealing to Jung about alchemy? He felt that he had stumbled upon the 'historical counterpart' to his psychology of the unconscious. 'The possibility of a comparison with alchemy and the uninterrupted intellectual chain back to Gnosticism, gave substance to my psychology' (ibid., p. 205). He became convinced that 'without history there can be no psychology, and certainly no psychology of the unconscious.' Whereas an ego-psychology might content itself with material drawn from personal life, Jung felt that dreams and neurotic symptoms 'need more than personal memories for their interpretation.'

Jung regarded his work on alchemy as the capstone of his career. It gave meaning and purpose to the second half of his life. If someone had told him before his mid-life transition that he would be spending the next thirty years of his life studying the psychology of alchemy, he would have laughed and dismissed the idea as preposterous. At that time he was a dedicated Freudian psychoanalyst, committed to teaching and spreading Freud's gospel. But the encounter with the archetypal symbols of the unconscious made all the difference to him. He emerged from that Nekyia a changed man. Like Goethe he felt that he was in the grip of that process of archetypal transformation which has gone on through the centuries. What Jung said of Goethe, he felt was also true of himself:

> He regarded his Faust as an *opus magnus* or *divinum*. He called it his 'main business,' and his whole life was enacted within the framework of this drama. Thus what was alive and active within him was a living substance, a suprapersonal process, the great dream of the *mundus archetypus* (archetypal world).
>
> I myself am haunted by the same dream, and from my eleventh year I have been launched upon a single enterprise which is my 'main business.' My life has been permeated

and held together by one idea and one goal: namely, to penetrate into the secret of the personality. Everything can be explained from this central point, and all my works relate to this one theme (ibid., p. 206).

After his mid-life crisis, Jung's basic attitude to life changed. He began to see himself as the servant of the psyche. His reference group was no longer medical psychology or psychoanalysis, but religion in the form of the psycho-spiritual quest which he called the individuation process. Since scientific psychology did not seem a relevant reference point to him any longer, he turned to oriental religions and the occult sciences for intellectual inspiration and support.

Some reflection on this change in Jung's values may help us illuminate the nature of the transformation he underwent at mid-life. What was at stake was Jung's ego-identity. Before his mid-life transition he had identified his ego with his rational mind and himself with his ego. In the course of his mid-life quest his ego identity became relativized and the Self emerged as the new center of his personality. From this deeper Self perspective, reason seemed less fundamental a value to Jung. He began to value religious and mystical experience over rational understanding. After his mid-life crisis, Jung agreed with Nietzsche that reason limps along rather helplessly as a handmaid behind experience, illuminating the path we have trod, but indicating little about where we must go. 'Rational understanding or intellectual formulation adds nothing to the experience of wholeness; at best it only facilitates its repetition,' Jung wrote (ibid., p. 217). In other words, after his mid-life crisis Jung felt that direct experience of the nouminous depths of the psyche was more important than intellectual analysis of the experience. Analysis, he felt, should be relied upon only when the path to original experience was blocked.

In his mid-life crisis Jung re-experienced aspects of his early childhood and reconnected with his early religious roots, to beliefs and values he had neglected or abandoned while he was an orthodox Freudian. Freud viewed religion as neurotic and infantile. Jung saw it as the highest achievement of human culture and the *sine qua non* of psychological health. Yet the imagery of traditional religion does not work for many modern persons, and Jung was one of these. His way was to develop the religion of the archetypes. Going into his own void he discovered his own riches there. This gave him a new symbolic context to replace the lost brotherhood of the psychoanalytic movement. Now he identified himself with what he saw as his true predecessors, the ancient Christian Gnostics. Later on, he was to view the medieval alchemists as the missing link between himself and the secret wisdom of the ancient Christian world.

In this chapter I have examined the process and pattern in Jung's mid-life transition. While similar in certain respects to the general pattern of mid-life crisis we have since come to understand through the studies of Jacques (1970), Sheehy (1976), Mayer (1978), and Levinson *et al.* (1978), Jung's experience was different in some respects and more intense in all respects than the mid-life transitions of most other people. Fortunately, most people do not have to risk a near psychotic breakdown in moving through the transition from early to middle adulthood.

Research indicates that the mid-life transition occurs for most people regardless of whether the individual succeeds or fails in his search for affirmation by society. The real issue seems to be what to do with the experience of disparity between what the individual may have gained from living within a particular life structure and what he now wants for himself. 'The sense of disparity between "what I've reached at this point" and "what it is I really want" instigates a soul searching for "what I really want" ' (Levinson *et al.*, 1978). This quest often leads to an experience of rebirth or life renewal.

While the general pattern of mid-life crisis is a common one, responses to it differ. The ancient Chinese character for 'crisis' also means 'opportunity.' From the example of Jung's life experience we can see that this period is a time of great opportunities for the development of the Self; it is also a period fraught with danger. Only a very strong person could have survived the psychic turmoil Jung experienced at mid-life. We know of others such as Nietzsche, Dylan Thomas, F. Scott Fitzgerald, and Vincent Van Gogh, who were unable to meet the demands of this period in their lives and who destroyed themselves or went insane.

One of the main characteristics of those who were able to profit from the experience of mid-life initiation, as Jung was, is the development of a positive relationship to non-ego aspects of the Self, such as the inner voice Jung called the 'daimon of creativity.' Writers and thinkers who successfully weathered the storm, such as Dante, Freud, Jung, Hesse, Mann, Frank Lloyd Wright, and Bertrand Russell, found that their later work had a depth and maturity of perspective that sprang from creative energies released in them from this perilous initiation experience. Jung felt that everything he accomplished in later life derived from his mid-life vision quest (Jung, 1961, p. 192).

Chapter 4
The development of Jung's theory of the individuation process in the second half of life

Having been given a biographical account of Jung's mid-life transition in the preceding chapter, now let us consider how Jung translated his experience into a scientific conceptual scheme and a therapeutic procedure. We will focus particularly on the essays he wrote during the decade after he emerged from his mid-life crisis, to consider how his developmental theory reflected and expressed his own life experience and his intellectual and cultural milieu.

In his memoirs Jung readily admitted the close connection between his psychological theory and his own personal experience.

> All my works, all my creative activity, has come from those initial fantasies and dreams which began in 1912 . . . . Everything that I accomplished in later life was already contained in them, although at first only in the form of emotions and images (Jung 1961, p. 192).

In fact, he felt a compulsion to convert his personal experience into scientific theory. 'My science was the only way I had of extricating myself from that chaos' (ibid.). He felt that if he had not objectified his imaginal experience he might have drowned in it. We have already seen how much care he took in trying to understand the meaning of every dream and fantasy image, every item of his psychic inventory, and to classify them scientifically. In the ensuing years Jung sought to 'realize them in actual life' and to embody them in his own theoretical and practical psychology (ibid.).

Jung presented his ideas and theories about personality development and the individuation process in a number of essays and in scattered places throughout his works written after his mid-life transition. It is neither possible nor necessary here to recapitulate all his arguments in each of these works. Instead I will present a brief summary of the main points in his theory. I will not present these ideas chronologically because it is more important to treat them logically. Nevertheless, to give the reader a sense of the progression of Jung's thought regarding various aspects of the individuation process, the titles and dates of original publication of the most important essays dealing with individuation are indicated in Table 1.

Table 1   Essays dealing with individuation

1916	*Septem Sermones ad Mortuos*	*Memories, Dreams, and Reflections,* Appendix
	'The transcendent function'	*CW**, vol. 8
	'The structure of the unconscious'	*CW*, vol. 7
	'The psychology of the unconscious'	*CW*, vol. 7
1921	*Psychological Types*	*CW*, vol. 6
1925	'Marriage as a psychological relationship'	*CW*, vol. 17
1926	'Analytical psychology and education'	*CW*, vol. 17
	'The significance of the unconscious in individual education'	*CW*, vol. 17
1928	*Two Essays in Analytical Psychology*	*CW*, vol. 7
1929	'The secret of the golden flower'	*CW*, vol. 13
1931	'The stages of life'	*CW*, vol. 8
1932	'The development of personality'	*CW*, vol. 17
1934	'The soul and death'	*CW*, vol. 8

*Collected Works.

Of course all of Jung's later works, such as those on psychology and alchemy, deal with the individuation process, but these are beyond the scope of this study. They are products of Jung's late adulthood and this study is focused on Jung's mid-life transition and the relation of his theory of adult development to his experience of this transition.

Most theories of human development have emphasized either physical, emotional, cognitive, or moral development. Jung's theory is exceptional and important because he was one of the first psychologists to consider the development of the person holistically as well as across the entire lifespan. In his theory of psychological types Jung distinguished between the basic opposite types, introvert and extravert. He also differentiated the human personality functions of sensation, feeling, thinking, and intuition, showing how these were differently expressed among introverts and extraverts. In Jung's view, the goal of human development was wholeness and balance among the four functions. Most importantly, Jung insisted that behind our ego-consciousness there is a natural process of differentiation and integration going on. The unconscious in this theory functions almost like an invisible hand guiding our lives. Jung believed that through the analysis of our dreams and fantasies we can discover this inner purpose and thereby find more meaning in our lives. In his view the discovery of this meaning was one of the main tasks of later life.

Jung and self-actualization theory

Before going into a discussion of Jung's theory of individuation in the second half of life, it may be helpful to compare and contrast his work briefly with some other theorists to put it in context. Jung's work differs radically from behaviorism and other psychological theories that view human conduct as a result of what comes to the individual from the outside (stimulus/response). That Jung was extremely critical of behaviorist views is evident from the following quotation:

> The disastrous idea that everything comes to the human psyche from outside and that it is born a *tabula rasa* is responsible for the erroneous belief that under normal circumstances the individual is in perfect order . . . . As a result of these prejudices, the individual feels totally

dependent on the environment and loses all capacity for introspection. In this way his code of ethics is replaced by a knowledge of what is permitted or forbidden or ordered (Jung, 1958, p. 267).

This mechanistic determinism was, Jung felt, the result of the excessively extraverted approach characteristic of most academic psychology. In his own work, characteristic of himself as an introvert, Jung sought to compensate for and to complement the one-sidedness of academic experimental psychology. Jung was sceptical of any psychological theory that pretended to be free of the 'personal equation.' He was critical of all theories that ignored the unconscious or denied the autonomy and self-directedness of the psyche.

Abraham Maslow (1970), developed a theory of self-actualization that bears comparison to Jung's ideas. Like Jung, Maslow emphasized the self-regulating, self-determining character of the person. Maslow divided human interests into D (deficiency) cognitions and B (being) cognitions. D cognition is selective apperception of a thing according to the needs of the cognizer. This cognition is self-interested and leads to a potentially exploitive relationship. B cognition, on the other hand, is a selfless striving toward a higher form of order and meaning rather than a striving to meet a need. In Maslow's hierarchy of human motives, 'self-actualization' is the highest motive and underlies B cognition.

While Maslow seems to have viewed self-actualization as a peculiarly human characteristic, Jung viewed the psyche as being part of the order of nature, and he insisted that self-actualization was characteristic of all living organisms. Such was his trust in nature and the natural healing processes in the psychological development of persons that Jung's watchword was 'Don't interfere.' It was his practice to observe extensive dream series in his patients in order to study the natural unfolding and development of the psyche.

The ethics of self-actualization goes back to the beginnings of Western civilization. According to Plato and Aristotle self-actualization consists in rendering explicit what one implicitly already is. Think of the words inscribed on the temple of Apollo at Delphi, 'know thyself,' and the words of the poet Pindar, 'become what you are.' The self that a man is required to discover and know is not his empirical person but his deeper self, of which his empirical self is a pale reflection. In this view every person is both his empirical actuality and his ideal possibility. According to ancient self-actualization ethics it is every person's primary responsibility first to discover the daimon within him and thereafter to live in accordance with it. Perfection is impossible. One can never fully actualize oneself in the world, but by living in truth to oneself, guided by one's daimon, one's unique perfection can be progressively approached (Norton, 1976).

Jung's theory of the individuation process in the second half of life is a variety of self-actualization theory. As such it is an ethical theory as much as a psychological theory. Jung acknowledged this and maintained that in the final analysis the determining factors in human growth to higher levels of being and self-actualization are the moral and spiritual values we espouse and our choices and decisions to act on these.

Jung's holistic viewpoint is normative. His views of the whole person as a self-actualizing system interacting with others in a cultural context is a more adequate way of viewing human beings and behavior than is a mechanistic reductionistic one. Jung evaluated the development of a person in terms of that person's balance and wholeness and the person's relation to his inner and outer worlds.

The transcendent function: prefiguration of the Self

Jung's essay, 'The transcendent function,' (1972b) written in 1916, offers an excellent example of his holistic approach. It also demonstrates how he translated his own personal experience into psychological theory. The task of psychotherapy, he said, was to overcome the dissociation between conscious and unconscious contents in the psyche and to bring the two into a dynamic interchange which he called a 'transcendent function.' This Archimedean point in the psyche is 'transcendent' of the polarities in the personality and makes a transition from one attitude to another possible. Like the notion of self-actualization, the 'transcendent function' is a normative, teleological concept.

Once having broken from Freud's alleged ethical neutrality, Jung had no compunctions about introducing a strongly ethical and teleological emphasis into his theorizing. For example, he suggested that the meaning of the transference lay not in its reduction to its infantile origins, but rather in its goals or final purpose, the object beyond itself through which it could be transcended. In Jung's view the analyst functioned for the psyche of his client rather like a transitional object (1972b). In time, and with experience, the client might grow beyond this infantile dependence on the analyst and come to rely more on his own inner images for guidance, as Jung himself had done.

A word must be said about the dialectical character of the transcendent function in Jungian theory. Echoing the notion of dialectics as a process moving from thesis to antithesis to synthesis, Jung argued that the symbolic process entails the constellation of opposites which are then transcended through the psyche's production of a 'living symbol' from the unconscious. Torn between thesis and antithesis, the ego finds in the middle ground its own counterpart, its unique means of expression, and 'it eagerly seizes upon this in order to be delivered from its division' (Jung, 1971, p. 479). This primordial living symbol is supposed to reconcile the polar opposites in the personality in a new synthesis.

Confrontation with the unconscious

In contacting the primordial symbols in the collective unconscious the individual is able to participate in something cosmic within himself, in the cosmos, and in the social collectivity. Whereas most people live in a state of unconscious participation, identified with, and undifferentiated from, the myths and symbols of the collectivity, it is possible to become individuated and self-actualized by disidentifying from these collective symbols and in discovering their symbolic analogues within oneself. In this case the collective symbols are not rejected, but are respected and reinterpreted, i.e., psychologized and internalized. Jung's essay on 'Transformation symbolism in the mass' (1958), originally published in 1954, is a good example of this process. In it, Jung indicates ways to personally connect with the psychological realities behind traditional Christian ritual and symbolism so that one develops a personal relationship with Christ viewed as a symbol of the Self.

For Jung the instinctive, archaic basis of the mind was 'a matter of plain objective fact.' This structure was 'more dependent on personal choice than was the inherited structure and functioning of the brain itself' (Jung, 1970b, p. 136), or any other organ, for that matter. Just as the body had its evolutionary history, which had left clear traces in the development of the embryo, so also did the psyche. Being a psycho-Lamarckian, like Freud, Jung believed that ontogeny recapitulated phylogeny psychically as well as physiologically. Collective symbolic thought corresponded, Jung maintained, to an initial phase of human thought, a time when man was not yet concerned with the domination of nature and the external world, and was turned inwards, seeking to express in myth the psychic discoveries resulting from this introversion. Jung found that particularly in later life, any introversion, though derived from the individual's personal history, was also bound to be tinged with the archaic history of the human race as well. In the intense regression and introversion of psychosis archaic features would become more pronounced. Thus, in contrast to most other psychologists of personality development Jung anchored individual development in the context of collective representations and images, in myths and symbols, in history and culture (ibid., p. 138).

Religion and individuation

In contrast to Freud and his followers who viewed religion as an infantile neurosis, an example of substitution of an idealized object for the real one which one cannot have, Jung viewed psychological development as closely related with moral and spiritual development. Jung found that for most of his patients healing and wholeness was usually accompanied by religious experiences of one kind or another. In his view religion was important to adult development because it affected the whole person where the essential processes of development took place, in the unconscious. Jung traced back to the unconscious the 'inner voice' so important to every religious person. 'Revelation,' Jung said 'is an opening of the depths of the human soul, a "laying bare," a psychological mode pure and simple, which says nothing about what else it could be. That lies outside the bounds of science' (Jung, 1958, p. 133). Jung spoke with the voice of experience having had his own private revelation from Philemon and other archetypal figures.

Whereas Freud set out to de-mythologize psychology, Jung and his followers re-mythologized psychology and re-evaluated the educational and therapeutic character of religion in psychological development. In fact, Jung felt that general conceptions of a spiritual nature were indispensible constituents of psychic life. Their relative absence in modern culture was a sign of decadence. The future of psychology, he felt, lay in rebuilding the lost connections between man and the cosmos that primitive man still understood, although in an archaic and infantile form, through his religious and cultural traditions and spiritual practices. Our task, Jung said, was to unlearn our manipulative and controlling attitudes and to rediscover our partnership with other creatures in the natural world and in our own souls. Mythology and religion contained deep psychological truths not embodied in modern scientific psychology. Jung sought to reconnect his patients with the religious traditions. In his practice, psychology became a kind of 'soul-making' (Hillman, 1975).

Psychological types and the problems of opposites

Jung's whole system of psychology as he developed it during these years was based on his own developmental experience. To demonstrate this point let us consider *Psychological Types* (Jung, 1971), published in 1921. It was the first major work Jung wrote after his self-analysis. In it, if we read between the lines, we can find many allusions to his own transformation and his discovery of the individuation process.

Jung's research into psychological types yielded the insight that every judgment made by an individual is conditioned by his personality type and that every point of view is necessarily relative. This led him to look for the unity which could compensate this diversity. He found it in the Chinese concept of the Tao, which he viewed as an image of the Self, the centerpoint transcending the conflict of opposites. He elaborated this point of view in his commentary on 'The secret of the golden flower,' (1967c), originally published in 1929, a Chinese Taoist alchemical text translated by his friend Richard Wilhelm. In his memoirs, after mentioning this text, Jung commented 'it was only after I had reached the central point in my thinking and in my researches, namely the concept of the *Self*, that I once more found my way back to reach out again to the world' (1961, p. 208). Thereafter, in the late 1920s he began to reach out again to the world. Another shift of direction or reversal of psychic energy was at hand, as Jung moved from extreme introversion back into a moderate extroversion. Throughout his life Jung continued to oscillate between these poles, but as the years went by the latitude of these oscillations diminished and he centered more in himself and his own psyche.

In *Psychological Types*, Jung observed that in the first half of life we tend to develop one aspect of our personality to a high degree. This becomes what Jung called our 'dominant function.' At a certain point the very thing that worked so well for us becomes a problem. Usually this occurs with a change in external or inner circumstances such as life transitions bring about. For example, while a young person is generally concerned with securing a place for himself in the world, Jung maintained that more mature people should know that their life task is not so much expansion and differentiation but integration.

One of the central concepts in *Psychological Types* is the principle of the opposites. In the philosophy of Heraclitus we find the term *enantiodromia* used to designate the play of opposites in the course of events – the view that everything that exists turns into its opposite. Jung adapted this notion for his psychological theory of human development:

> I use the term *enantiodromia* for the emergence of the unconscious opposite in the course of time. This characteristic phenomenon practically always occurs when an extreme one-sided tendency dominates conscious life; in time an equally powerful counter-position is built up, which first inhibits the conscious performance and subsequently breaks through the conscious control (Jung, 1971, p. 426).

As examples of *enantiodromia* Jung cited the conversion of St Paul, the self-identification of the sick Nietzsche with Christ, and the transformation of Swedenborg from an erudite scholar into a mystic visionary. *Enantiodromia* plays a role in society as well; if a society is overdeveloped rationally it is likely to run into its opposite, the irrational devastation of culture (Jung, 1971, p. 185).

The problem of opposites usually comes up in the second half of life when all the illusions we projected upon the world gradually come back to haunt us. 'The energy streaming back from these manifold relationships falls into the unconscious and activates all the things we had neglected to develop' (Jung, 1966b, p. 59). 'To the man in the second half of life the development of the function of the opposites lying dormant in the unconscious means a renewal' (ibid., p. 61).

Jung viewed life teleologically. Like a projectile flying to its goal, life ends in death. Even its ascent and its zenith are only steps and means to this goal. He compared the course of life to the parabola of a projectile which, disturbed from its initial state of rest, rises and then returns to a state of repose. However, the psychological curve of life does not always conform to this analogy. Sometimes although the projectile ascends biologically (maturity), psychologically (developmentally) it lags behind. We straggle behind our years (Jung, 1972a, p. 406).

To demonstrate his point Jung cited the example of an American businessman who had consulted him. He had been very successful and had decided to retire when he was in his early forties. He bought a lovely country estate and planned to lead a gay social life. However, the energy which should have been available now would not flow towards these entertaining prospects. He began brooding over peculiar vague sensations in his body. In a few weeks he was plunged into a complete nervous collapse. From a healthy man of bounding energy he had become a peevish child. He then consulted a physician who recognized his symptoms and told him there was nothing wrong with him but lack of work. He returned to his former position, but found to his immense disappointment that now the business no longer interested him. His energy could not be forced back into the old grooves. His condition became even worse. 'His creative genius rose up, as it were, in revolt against him; and just as before he had built up great organizations in the world, so now his daimon spun equally subtle systems of hypochondriacal delusion that completely annihilated him' (Jung, 1966b, p. 52).

Jung interpreted this case in terms of the law of *enantiodromia*. This energy that had been withdrawn from the business now needed to find a new direction. He tried to interest the man in his dreams. But it was too late. He was already a moral ruin. This man had a daimon, a fate but he refused to listen to it and he was destroyed. Whereas he had differentiated his thinking function to a high degree, the rest of him had remained inert and underdeveloped. Jung told him that he needed to contact and develop this 'inferior' side of himself if he wanted to live. That was the message his depression contained. Jung's arguments fell on deaf ears. He was already too far gone (Jung, 1966b, pp. 51–2).[1]

Dissolution of the persona

Despite the fact that the path was fraught with dangers, Jung maintained that for the person seeking to follow the course of full individuation there was no other way than to take on the task of a direct confrontation with the unconscious. What he had done, Jung felt, others must also do. Individuation entailed abandoning the comfortable security of identification of who I am with what I do, our familiar personal and social roles which Jung called the *persona* or social mask. For example, Jung's persona was being a physician or psychiatrist. Dissolution of this persona was necessary for development because the persona is simply a segment of the collective psyche. Such a mask only simulates our individuality, but it does not express it. We discover in analysis that what we thought was individual and unique with us is really collective, an internalized false self system.

Dissolution of the persona can be terrifying. It often leads to a release of disturbing wild fantasies, or to fearful feelings of extreme vulnerability. The person may attempt to flee from the encounter with the unconscious back into the familiar security of his persona repudiating the unconscious as madness or a mistake. Alternatively, he might fall into a complete identification with the unconscious in which the ego is swamped and individual identity disappears. Often images of incest come up. Jung interpreted the latter as indicating a desire for re-birth, for a return to the material source of new life. Though the 'Night Sea Journey' is difficult, based on his own experience, Jung felt it to be the necessary symbolic expression of life transition and a prerequisite for development to higher stages of being and consciousness.

Individuation and collectivity

In Jung's view the developmental task of adulthood is individuation, that process whereby we become who we really are (Jung, 1966b, p. 171). Individuation entails the progressive integration of the unconscious Self in the life of the time- and space-bound individual. 'The aim of individuation,' Jung said, was to 'divest the Self of the false wrappings of the persona, on the one hand, and of the suggestive power of primordial images, on the other' (ibid., p. 174). Paradoxically, in becoming ourselves, in becoming who we really are, we also express one of the many facets of the primordial reality of the psyche, which crystallizes its own being in this way. Thus, individual human development in Jung's psychological theory, is connected with human and even cosmic evolution. In this conceptual framework the individual is no longer isolated and alone; instead he becomes the 'makeweight' who through his consciousness tips the scales of human history.

Jung viewed 'individuation' and 'collectivity' as a pair of opposites. Critics of Jung have objected that he had no sense of society, that individuation takes place in a vacuum. This is a false criticism. In Jung's view individuation is only possible to the extent that an individual can purchase his individuation at the cost of an equivalent work for the benefit of the collective, society. Only those who have paid the price to society through their own initiative can go on to the further reaches of individuation.

In an essay written during the First World War, Jung discussed the conflicts of duty and responsibility to Self and society that are likely to occur in the process of individuation.

> Individuation cuts one off from personal conformity and hence from collectivity. That is the guilt which the individual leaves behind him for the world, that is the guilt he must endeavour to redeem. He must offer a ransom in place of himself, that is, he must bring forth values which are an equivalent substitute for his absence in the collective personal sphere. Without this production of values,

final individuation is immoral and – more than that – suicidal. The man who cannot create values should sacrifice himself consciously to the spirit of collective conformity (Jung, 1977, p. 450).

In other words, only the person who can create objective values which can be recognized by society, has the right to individuation, which is justified only so long as substitute values are created by the individuating person. 'Not only has society a right,' said Jung, 'it also has a duty to condemn the individual if he fails to create equivalent values, for he is a deserter.'

He who would individuate must fight against the tyranny of the majority and the banalities of mass society as well as against the contents of the collective unconscious. 'It is in the achievement of victory over the collective that the true values lie' (Jung, 1966b, p. 174).

It is not surprising that in his book *Psychological Types* (1971) Jung emphasizes the differences and complementarity between extraverts and introverts, between those who adapt more easily to the outer world or to the inner world. Jung himself was an introverted type. His therapeutic process reflected his character and temperament. In fact, Jungian therapy may be viewed as a kind of socialization for introversion. While the goal of Jungian therapy is balance and wholeness, the emphasis in much of Jungian work seems to be on developing a positive and fruitful relationship with the figures of our dream and fantasy life as much or more than on adaptation to the outer world. This inner emphasis both reflects Jung's own experience and character and his view that in later life our principal task is inner development to complement the emphasis on mastery and achievement characteristic of early adulthood for most people in our culture. Perhaps for this reason Jung's psychology has been particularly appealing to women. Jung surrounded himself with women disciples during the second half of his life, in contrast to Freud whose chief disciples were mostly men.

The moral dimension of individuation

The individuation process requires the collaboration of the ego and the unconscious. Whereas in the early stage of analysis the ego might take a back seat, in the later synthetic stage the ego must take a leading role. Furthermore, we can learn to converse with our inner figures, to interpret our dreams and fantasies, to listen to the wisdom of the body, etc., but all of this will not really serve to further our own development if we do not draw the conclusions and make the choices and the effort through which we actualize these possibilities and embody them in our lives. Unless the unconscious material is not only analyzed and interpreted but also integrated into the conscious life of the subject, the encounter with the unconscious is unlikely to have any positive lasting effect. As Jung had discovered from his own experience, 'the images of the unconscious place a great responsibility upon a man. Failure to understand them, or a shirking of ethical responsibility, deprives him of his wholeness and imposes a painful fragmentariness on his life' (Jung, 1961, p. 193). 'Analysis is not enough; it is the moral factor which is decisive in health and disease' (ibid., p. 195). In stressing the role of will and moral choice, Jung differed from the mainstream of academic and medical psychology in his time. Perhaps it was his own deep roots in the Protestant church that impelled him to emphasize moral factors in health and illness as he did.

Jung's interpretation of the tasks of adult development hinged on his differentiation between personal (or individual) and transpersonal (or collective) aspects of psychic life. Development requires the assimilation of transpersonal collective unconscious elements into personal ego consciousness. However, this process is fraught with potential dangers. A person might be filled with a sense of superiority upon encountering the unconscious or he might feel ashamed at harboring such strange thoughts and images in himself. Jung often cited Nietzsche as a prime example of a person who made the mistake of identifying with his 'mana personality,'

Zarathustra, and became unbalanced afterwards. The task of individuation was to integrate the collective or transpersonal elements in the unconscious without succumbing to either inflation or feelings of inferiority. For example, in the course of analysis one might discover one's divine nature or feel oneself to be a channel of divine revelation. According to Jung, what one should do in such situations is to acknowledge the feeling and then to let go of it and come back to one's own center. Acknowledgment of archetypal images and integration of them into ego consciousness enables one to realize more of the Self in one's daily life. This is part of the process of Self-actualization, of making the potentialities of the Self actual in one's life.

In his seminal essay on 'The stages of life' (1972a), written in 1932, Jung observed that the 'process of individuation' in the second half of life is often ushered in by an experience of emptiness and depression. It entails a recognition that we contain within us not only an ego, but also a deeper Self which manifests itself through various archetypal figures. Recognition and integration of these archetypes generally leads to a widening of consciousness and increased creativity in later life. But this new state of being is often bitterly opposed and resisted by the ego, that monarch who has heretofore ruled the personality unchallenged. In the afternoon of our lives, Jung believed, we must accept a gradual waning of our energies or at least a shift in direction, experiencing 'the reversal of all the ideals and values that were cherished in the morning' (Jung, 1972a, p. 397). The ego goals of early adulthood, whether achieved or not, become inappropriate, and must be replaced by Self goals as we enter middle and late adulthood.

The ego and the Self

What stands out as most radical in Jung's theory is his relativization of the ego in relation to the Self. In all other Western scientific theories of human development, the ego is viewed as the goal of human development throughout the life cycle. For Jung, on the other hand, the ego, though very important is neither the center nor the goal of human development, which is the realization of the Self, or wholeness. For this reason I call Jung's psychology a Self-psychology rather than an ego-psychology.

Whereas most other psychologists use the words 'ego' and 'Self' interchangeably, Jung differentiated the 'ego' from the 'Self.' He defined the ego more narrowly than most ego-psychologists, viewing it as 'only the center of my field of consciousness' (Jung, 1971, p. 425). The ego is not identical with the totality of the psyche, which also includes the unconscious. On the other hand, the Self, is defined by Jung as 'the whole range of psychic phenomena in man,' which resembles his definition of the psyche as 'the totality of all psychic processes, conscious as well as unconscious.' The Self 'expresses the unity of the personality as a whole.' However, since the total personality can be only in part conscious, on account of its unconscious component, Jung maintained that his notion of the Self was 'a transcendental concept,' encompassing 'both the experienceable and the inexperienceable or the not yet experienced.' Nevertheless, as experienced, the symbols of the Self, such as the mandala, possess a highly numinous quality and can lead the person forward to higher stages of integration in his own development.

Studying the patterns of behavior in animal species, Jung pointed out that a psychoid *proto-image*, darkly unconscious and yet purposeful, guides the development of every organism; and in the human species, this *proto-image* is the Self. The Self represents the basic realities of human nature, the potentialities and the limits of man's life; and since it is an image that eventually takes a psychological form, the Self is experienced as a symbol of the meaning and the goal of man's existence. In a variety of archetypal forms that cover the virtually unlimited symbolism of redemption, the Self draws man forward by relating his activities to larger contexts of life beyond his immediate knowledge. It leads man beyond himself and it does this necessarily because the fundamental psychoid nature of the human species requires an attempt at spiritual transcendence. In Jung's view, in order to fulfill his nature, man must reach beyond his own life to an experience of something in which he is encompassed but which he can never define. He may seek it in the heavens and find it there, but if he finds it, it is because a mystery of life has revealed itself to him out of the depths of the Self.

'The Self that encompasses me,' Jung wrote, 'also encompasses many others . . . . It does not belong to me nor is it characteristically mine, but it is universal. Paradoxically, it is the quintessence of the individual, and at the same time a continuum for all mankind.' As a psychological term, the Self represents the finite depth and magnitude of human personality. At its furthest reaches it touches the deepest ground of Being where man experiences the boundlessness of the soul. Thus the term 'the Self' is both psychological and parapsychological, pointing beyond psychology to levels of experience that transcend the ordinary range of intellectual understanding.

According to Jung, the undiscovered Self is always with us, even in childhood, trying to make itself manifest through our lives in a process of growing self-realization. To make the journey of individuation, the journey into wholeness, is to discover and live out the meaning of the Self through choice of awareness of the hidden movement of non-ego forces in the psyche. It is a journey of change and transformation, of symbolic deaths and rebirths, on many different levels of our being. The way of individuation contains its own inner blueprint and is self-correcting; only what is really one's Self has the power to heal.

The Self, Jung says, is 'as it were a virtual point midway between conscious and unconscious,' between ego and non-ego (1958, p. 263). It acts as a center of gravity that holds the fragmentary parts of the psyche together. It is also the source of dynamic energy out of which consciousness is born. In Jung's view this Self is not only the source and groundwork of the personality, but also the power that seeks to become manifest through the choices and experiences of that same ego to which it has given birth. In other words, this non-ego force needs the ego in order to fulfill itself in a meaningful relation not only to the world but also to all the unborn or lost potentials of the whole man.

> Human nature shrinks definitely back from becoming conscious. What, however, drives [man] onward toward consciousness is the Self. . . . On the one hand, to become conscious . . . is a conscious act of will on the part of the ego, on the other hand it is a spontaneous manifestation of the Self which has existed forever (ibid., p. 263).

The ego stands in relation to the Self as the moved to the mover, or as object to subject, because the determining factors which radiate out from the Self surround the ego on all sides and are supraordinate to it.

In Jung's view the Self has an eternal character; it is preexistent to consciousness and is the father and creator of the ego. The Self, like the unconscious, is an *a priori* existence out of which the ego evolves. It is an unconscious prefiguration of the ego. 'It is not I who create myself, rather I happen to myself' (ibid., p. 259). In Jung's view the superego is a substitute for experience of the Self:

> So long as the Self is unconscious, it corresponds to Freud's superego and is a source of perpetual moral conflict. If it is withdrawn from projection, however, and is no longer identical with public opinion then one is truly one's own yea and nay. The Self then functions as a union of opposites and thus constitutes the most immediate experience of the Divine which it is psychologically possible to imagine (ibid., p. 261).

The Self can only be comprehended by us in particular acts, but remains concealed from us as a whole because it is more comprehensive than we are. All we can do is draw conclusions from the bits of the Self that we can experience.

Integration or humanization of the Self is initiated from the conscious side by our making ourselves aware of our selfish aims. We examine our motives and try to form an accurate and complete picture of our own nature. This act of self-reflection is a recollection, a gathering together of all the things in us that have never been properly related, a coming to terms with one's self, with a view to achieving full consciousness. This bringing together of our scattered parts is both a conscious choice of the ego and at the same time a 'spontaneous manifestation of the Self.' Individuation thus appears to be both a synthesis of previously scattered particles and the revelation of something which already existed unconsciously before the ego (ibid., p. 263).

While ego-psychologists talk of tasks, mastery, and adaptation to the world, Jung, dealing with the subtle nuances of the phenomenology of the psyche, spoke more of symbolic processes, and utilized techniques of visualization, drawing, dance, and dream work to evoke them. He was aware of the need for balance in the personality and utilized these techniques to produce balance in his patients as he did with himself.

The philosophical background of Jung's theory

Although Jung found little support for his holistic notion of the Self in Western ego-psychology, he recognized that his idea of the Self paralleled the notion of the image of God within the soul in Western religious thought and the notion of the Atman in Eastern thought. The parallels of Jung's conception of the 'Collective Unconscious' or 'Objective Psyche,' as he sometimes called it, and the notion of *Geist* (Mind or Spirit) fashionable in the Europe of Jung's youth are also obvious. In a sense Jung was elaborating a phenomenology of the objective psyche not unlike Hegel's account of the unfolding and development of consciousness in his *Phenomenology of the Mind* (Hegel, 1967). In Jung's worldview the individuation of each person is also the self-actualization of the ultimate world principle, whether this be called psyche, God, Tao, Atman, mind or Spirit. As a scientist, however, he was careful to maintain that he was only describing what appeared to be the structure and dynamics of the psyche. His deeper philosophical and religious views come through much more clearly in his posthumously published memoirs than in his *Collected Works*, but these beliefs and values must be taken into account in any consideration of Jung's theory of human development.

Jung felt that the deep abiding truths mankind needs for survival lie buried within us and have been available to mankind throughout human history. When we look at history, he wrote, we see only what happens on the surface, and even this is distorted in the faded mirror of tradition. What has really been happening eludes our glance for the true historical event lies deeply buried, experienced by all and observed by none. The so-called 'great events of world history' were 'profoundly unimportant,' Jung thought. 'In the last analysis the essential thing is the life of the individual. This alone makes history.' In Jung's view, history is the process of working through social as well as individual polarities. A dialectical interplay of the opposites leads to the reconciliation and transformation of differences into new higher syntheses. With Jung we seem to have arrived at a psychologized version of Hegel's objectification of spirit in history. To fully understand individual human development it is necessary to understand the larger primal structure of which the development of each individual is a part.

It is even possible to wed Jungian and Marxian theory for they complement each other and both derive from the German idealist tradition. The difference is that whereas Marx substituted history for *Geist*, Jung substituted psyche as the subject of the historical process. The dialectic is moved forward in Marx's view through class struggle, in Jung's view through the polaristic nature of the psyche. Jung's dialectic unfolds as one element in life generates its opposite and the tension between these opposite develops a new transcendent function, a uniting symbol between and beyond these opposites.

If one were to point to a single overriding theme running through Jung's writings it would be his concern to reveal the unfolding of the objective psyche (collective unconscious) in the lives of modern individuals and in the works of art and culture produced by humanity through the ages. Jung's major discovery was the reality and autonomy of psychic facts. His own confrontation with the unconscious had taught him that the psyche is a reality *sui generis*, a dimension of human experience that cannot be understood if reduced or explained in terms of extrapsychic factors such as biology, society, history, or even theology. His cosmic humanism led him to look for the universal, eternal themes that lay within not only the dreams of his modern patients but in human cultural history as well. His temperament led him to look for the universal behind the particular and the transpersonal through the personal.

Jung's model of adult development

Jung's major contribution to adult developmental psychology was to expand our understanding of personality development in middle adulthood and to present the broad outlines of a life-span developmental perspective at a time when most theories of human development still assumed adolescence to be the last developmentally given transition. While it was acknowledged that significant change could occur during adulthood, usually such change in the personality of an individual was attributed to remarkable *external* events such as dramatic successes or failures, severe trauma or illness, intensive psychotherapy, religious conversion, or major societal changes such as war, revolution, depression, or prosperity. Jung was the first psychologist to propose that developmental changes in the personality were to be expected and that these were initiated through an *internal* dynamic in the psyche which could be understood through a person's dreams and fantasy images.

According to Jung's model of human development, in

childhood and adolescence the ego is brought into being and is firmly established. As a person enters young adulthood he faces the task of creating the material and familial founda- tions for his later life. Personality, which develops over the course of a person's entire life, in Jung's view, 'is an *adult ideal*,' whose conscious realization through individuation is the aim of human development in the second half of life. In short, Jung maintained that a new process of *internal* development begins at mid-life, giving a different quality to the second half of life than had characterized the first half. Under favorable conditions, it is possible at mid-life to come to know one's self more deeply than before, and to begin giving more attention to the archetypal structures, which Jung viewed as the inner source of personality development, self-definition, wisdom, and personal creativity.

In the course of individuation a person can begin to deal with, and at least partially overcome, the great polarities which so often produce a splitting in the self and in our lives in early adulthood. A person must now come to terms with the *Animus/anima syzgy* – the archetypal, contrasexual figure – and thereby transcend the polarity of masculine and feminine that often so divides us in early adulthood. We can become more aware of the shadow, the archetypal figure containing those personal qualities that were repressed under the influence of our consciously held, socially programmed beliefs and values. We can confront more directly the twin archetypes of *puer* and *senex* (Hillman, 1968). In its pure form the *puer* represents birth, youthful potential, energy, unlimited possibility without weight, structure or constraint, flight, ascension, adventure, and often a heroic, tragic death. At the other extreme, the *senex* represents aging, dying, stasis, structure without energy, reason without joy, delibera- tion without action. In the successive eras of our lives there must be a changing balance and integration of this two- sided archetype.

The archetypes are, so to say, multiple seeds within the psyche. Most of them remain dormant through early adult- hood. Through the process of individuation in the second half of life, as a man nourishes the archetypal figures and gives them a more valued place in his life, they will evolve and enrich his life in ways hardly dreamed of in youth. As a man approaches old age, the archetype of the wise old man may guide and inspire him to become a wise old man himself. In any case this archetype connects us with our own inner knowingness, our own wisdom.

Jung likened the life cycle to the arc which the sun seems to describe on the horizon during the course of the day. Like the sun rising from the sea, at birth we emerge from our mother's womb, to grow through childhood passing through the transition of adolescence into young adulthood. At mid-life we face another developmentally given transition as we pass into middle adulthood, and enter the second half of life. As we approach old age we face another transition, parallel to adolescence, the late life transition. Thus, Jung divided the human life cycle into four eras, as portrayed in Figure 2. In his writings he said relatively little about childhood and old age; his principal interest was in middle adulthood and particularly in the dynamics of the mid-life transition, and its consequence and potentialities for creativity and wholeness in later life.

Jung believed that each season of life has its own particular character, value, and developmental tasks. 'A human being would certainly not grow to be seventy or eighty years old if this longevity had no meaning for the species,'

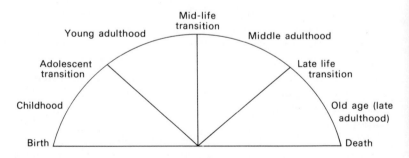

Figure 2   The human life cycle, showing major life transitions

he said. The afternoon of life has just as much significance as the morning, but it is different. It is neurotic, Jung said, to try to carry the psychology of childhood and youth into later life, to resist the imperatives of one's advancing years. 'We cannot live the afternoon of life according to the program of life's morning,' Jung said, 'for what in the morning was true will at evening have become a lie' (Jung, 1972b, p. 396). 'Whoever carried over into the afternoon the law of the morning . . . must pay with damage to his soul.'

Jung found that in later life spiritual and cultural values become increasingly important, especially as a person's physical energy and abilities begin to wane and friends and family members are lost. He believed that 'a spiritual goal that points beyond the purely natural man and his worldly existence is an absolute necessity for the health of the soul.' Such a spiritual goal provides us with 'an Archimedean point from which alone it is possible to lift the world off its hinges and to transform the natural state into a cultural one' (ibid., p. 398).[2] These spiritual goals need not be limited to the ones propagated by organized religions, however, through one's dreams and fantasy life one might discover one's own inner daimon, or guiding spirit, one's own calling, and one's own heartfelt values.

In this chapter I have attempted to show how Jung succeeded in using his fantasy and dream images and parapsychological experiences as a source for his own creativity, particularly after his mid-life crisis. Through an analysis of his writings on adult development and the individuation process, as well as on psychological types, I have shown how Jung moved from his own subjective experience – first expressed in his own private drawings and esoteric wisdom writings which he copied by hand in Gothic spirit into his 'red book' – to more objective scientific prose. I also discussed the way in which Jung translated his own experience of his fantasy and dream images into a systematic technique of mental imagery work. Since Jung did this, mental imagery work has become a common practice in many schools of psychotherapy and stress reduction from psychosynthesis to biofeedback, Gestalt therapy, and autogenic training, as well as in the Intensive Journal twilight imagery work of Ira Progoff (1977). Jung was a pioneer in this burgeoning field.

I attempted to show how Jung moved from the personal to the transpersonal, archetypal, collective dimension of human consciousness and culture. What is unique about Jung, in my opinion, is that he did not reject or invalidate the insights of Freud and other pioneers in depth psychology, rather he accepted their ideas as valid, at the level to which he felt they were relevant, and he incorporated them into his practice when he felt they were appropriate (1966b). With Jung the patient always came first, before any conceptual framework or scientific theory.

I believe that Jung's emphasis on the archetypes of the collective unconscious, those archetypal universals of human development, complement and supplement the personal emphasis of psychoanalysis, ego developmental psychology, and humanistic–existential psychology. In my opinion, the recognition that each life is totally singular and unique and that each of us in his or her experience is also realizing the pattern of human life – a pattern realized an infinite number of times before us – is an immensely liberating one, and it leads to a kind of serenity we can see in the old Jung, as reflected in his memoirs.

> My life is what I have done, my scientific work; the one is inseparable from the other. The work is the expression of my inner development; for commitment to the contents of the unconscious forms the man and produces his transformations. My works can be regarded as stations along my life's way.
>
> All my writings may be considered tasks imposed from within; their source was a fateful compulsion. What I wrote were things that assailed me from within myself. I permitted the spirit that moved me to speak out.

A creative person has little power over his own life. He is not free. He is captive and driven by his daimon . . . . The daimon of creativity has ruthlessly had its way with me . . . I have been impelled to say what no one wants to hear.

I am satisfied with the course my life has taken. . . . Much might have been different if I myself had been different. But it was as it had to be; for all came out because I am as I am (Jung, 1961, p. 397).

In his old age Jung experienced himself as enacting the archetype of the sage, the wise old man like Lao-tzu. His sense of connection with the archetypes gave him a sense of groundedness and enabled him to place his personal experience in a universal transpersonal context. The individual Jung allowed himself to become the spokesman of the objective psyche (collective unconscious) through the medium of his daimon.

Chapter 5
Conclusion

Now that we have reviewed the significant events and crises in Jung's adult life, and have considered the ways in which his theory of the individuation process in the second half of life reflected and expressed his own lived experience, it is time to assess the strengths and weaknesses of his theory and to relate it to contemporary adult developmental psychology. Jung's major contribution to developmental psychology in the 1920s and 1930s was to add the collective archetypal perspective and to demonstrate that personality development continues throughout the life cycle.

It is important to remember, however, that Jung was a clinically oriented psychiatrist, not a developmental psychologist.[1] His principle concern was to understand 'the secret of the personality' (Jung, 1961, p. 206) and to understand 'what actually takes place inside of the mentally ill' (ibid., p. 114). From his own life and from his clinical experience he came to understand a great deal about the processes and patterns of adult personality development, but his purpose was not the study of adult development as such. By choice he specialized in working with people who faced problems of adaptation to the changes of adult life as they grew older. Thus, his theory of the individuation process was developed as a response to these problems and was based on his own experience. He had no intention of articulating a general theory of adult development because he began from the premise that each case is different; each person is unique. He maintained that he was simply describing the phenomenology of the psyche. His generalizations regarding the individuation process relate to the formal structures, not to the particular contents or sequence of images. Having made the journey himself he then suggested that others might very likely encounter similar forms in their own healing journeys. In short, Jung did not begin his interpretation of adult development with a scientific hypothesis which he set out to test or prove. He began from his own experience and that of his patients; his theory of the individuation process was developed in order to account for and systematize his experience.

The strengths of Jung's theory

In reviewing the entire corpus of Jung's work, with an eye to assessing and evaluating its relevance to adult developmental psychology, I have found a number of ideas, concepts, and theoretical constructs which can be applied to adult development. Rather than attempt to detail all of these here, I have consolidated them under the rubric of eight perspectives that are characteristic of Jung's work. In my opinion these perspectives offer a broad foundation for the beginnings of a holistic developmental psychology, which will be discussed at the end of this chapter.

1 *Life-cycle perspective.* In his essay 'The stages of life' (1972a), originally published in 1932, Jung presented a rough outline map of the phases and transitions of the human life cycle. He stressed the transitions of adolescence, mid-life, and the late adult transition to old age. In this pioneering work, Jung argued that the task of life's afternoon is integration and synthesis of the Self, while the task of life's morning is active adaptation to the external world. In other essays on 'The development of personality' (1964a), originally published in 1932, and 'Marriage as a psychological relationship' (1964b), originally published in 1925, Jung noted that polarities such as masculine/feminine and youth/age exist

throughout the individual's life, but the balance shifts as we progress through the life cycle, and there is often a reversal of values and a re-evaluation of our marital and vocational commitments at mid-life.

2 *Typological perspective.* In his work *Psychological Types* (1971), Jung articulated a complex typological theory based on the fundamental polarity, introvert/extravert. He interpreted the basic functions of the personality in terms of the quadrinity: sensation, feeling, thinking, and intuition. In *Psychological Types*, Jung suggested some important implications of his typology for understanding patterns of human development through the life cycle. He maintained that in the course of early life people develop one personality function to a greater extent than the other functions. From mid-life on through the second half of life the task of development is to achieve a balance, harmony and wholeness in the personality through developing the underdeveloped functions. In Jung's typological model each personality type, such as 'introverted thinking type' or 'extraverted sensation type,' is said to develop in different ways in the course of the life cycle. Type thus becomes an important consideration in assessing developmental levels, and each person must be evaluated in comparison with others of his or her own type rather than being measured against any general norm.

3 *Comparative cultural perspective.* In Jung's view personality develops within specific cultural contexts and traditions. His relativistic perspective on personality development was fortified and confirmed from his experiences in his journeys to the United States, various European countries, North and Central Africa, and India. Jung consciously made trips to visit the blacks in a mental hospital in Washington, DC and Pueblo Indians on a reservation in New Mexico, for example, in order to evaluate cross-culturally and racially whether the patterns of thought and behavior he had observed in his patients in the Burgholzli Mental Hospital in Switzerland

were universal or culturally conditioned. In particular, Jung was interested in cross-cultural comparative studies of mythology, images, and symbols.[2]

4 *Mythic/religious perspectives.* Like Victor Frankl (1966), Abraham Maslow (1968, 1971), Peter Koestenbaum (1978), James F. T. Bugental (1976), Erich Fromm (1951), Rollo May (1976), and James Ogilvy (1977), not to mention a host of Jungian psychologists or those who have been directly influenced by Jung, Jung stressed the fundamental importance of the will to meaning in our lives. In his work with patients he attempted to help them to find their own myths to live by. In fact, he often said that any meaning is better than no meaning at all. In his view the spiritual and religious traditions of the past provided the guidelines for human development for most people until the modern age. In fact one might say that Jung's approach to adult development through individuation was created at least in part to fill the gap left in people's lives by the decline of organized religion. It has had a particularly strong appeal among lapsed or tepid Christians. In any case Jung maintained that in all cases the solution to problems of adaptation to the changes of later life entailed some kind of religious experience. He related the individuation process to spiritual traditions in the East and West, thereby giving his patients a sense that their own personal dramas could be connected to a larger universal human drama. He found that mythic stories and images give us a larger framework within which to observe and interpret our own individual development.

5 *Archetypal perspective.* In Jung's theory and practice, individual development is related to collective archetypal structures which shape the development process. Jung discovered the healing power of archetypal images and symbols in his own experience as well as in his clinical practice. His symbolic and imaginal orientation has important implications for anyone concerned with adult development and personality change. Whereas many other theories

of adult development have stressed relationship to the outer world as an indication of development, Jung showed that very often patterns of outer adaptation only change with or after the guiding images and archetypal dominants in the unconscious have altered.

Let me cite an example from Jung's discussion of the anima (inner feminine figure) in his book *Aion* (1974). There Jung speaks of how a man's energy may be drawn backwards into the archetypal Great Mother thus holding him back from facing the tasks of the next stage in his development. To advance forward in life this man must dissolve the power of the mother complex, and must be 'faithless' to the reigning mother *imago*. He needs all his masculine courage and resolution when it comes to throwing his whole being into the scales of life. A Freudian might interpret this situation as the Oedipal complex, which, of course on one level it is. Jung pushes it deeper into the archetypal dimension, the myth of the sacred marriage of mother and son, which illustrates the role of archetypes in guiding, facilitating, or impeding development. Jung's approach to this age old problem is to heal like with like, to dissolve the projection and induce an archetypal shift from the mother/son archetypal polarity to the man/woman polarity. Jung shows the patient that in the realm of his psyche there is an imago not only of the mother but also of the daughter, the sister, the beloved, the goddess, and the whore. This inner feminine figure, the anima, his image of woman, stands for those qualities in himself that he must now own. The dominant image shifts when properly amplified and interpreted and made conscious, freeing the man's energy to make further development possible.

6 *Dialectical perspective.* Jung was fascinated with polarities probably in part because of his own split nature. He viewed development and the transformation of psychic energy as being the result of interaction among polarities in the psyche, such as male/female, light/dark, individual/collective, etc. He found that developmental work with any

one polarity usually opened out into other polarities. In his view, dialectical development conflicts within the psyche are transcended when both sides of the polarity are owned and acknowledged. In the course of the individuation process, in Jung's view, there is a gradual shift in the center of the personality from the ego to the Self, but neither side of this polarity is ever abolished; they remain in dialectical interplay. The same holds true for the polarity individual/collective: we exist in a balancing field in which one or another element predominates at any time, but the field is a dynamic one in continual movement. Jung probably drew his dialectical perspective as much from Chinese Taoism as from German idealist philosophy. His dialectical perspective led him to think holistically.

7 *Holistic systems perspective.* Jung was a holistic thinker, who was predisposed to place individual elements within the context of larger structures and systems. His notion of the Self is a good example. He viewed it as a system-integrating structure in interaction with other living systems. Health, in his view, was homeostasis, balance within the system. Jung was receptive to the new physics and a systems view of reality partially because of his interest in Taoism, with its notion of reality as a dynamic interchange between Yin and Yang elements (Capra, 1975).

Jung believed that just as the physical organism cannot be fully understood by analyzing it in terms of its parts, so the properties and functions of the psyche cannot be understood by reducing the psyche to isolated elements. He thought of the human organism as a patterned whole involving physical, emotional, cognitive, social, and spiritual patterns. The individual organism is an integral part of interdependent and interacting larger systems.[3]

8 *Practical perspective.* Jung's approach to psychology was eminently practical. He considered each person in the round, in the context of his or her family and social worlds. His aim, he maintained was 'the best possible understanding

of life as we find it in the human soul' (1964c, p. 92). The purpose of analytical psychology was, he said, 'the better adaptation of human behavior' on two fronts: 'firstly to external life – profession, family, society – and secondly to the vital demands of his own nature.' Neglect of either imperative would lead to illness, Jung believed. He noted that not everyone who falls ill does so merely because he cannot meet the demands of the outside world, but rather because he does not know how to use his external adaptedness for the good of his most personal and intimate life and how to bring it to the right pitch of development (ibid., p. 93). Jung was concerned with why people fail to adapt to life. His psychology was a 'practical science,' not investigating 'for investigation's sake, but for the immediate purpose of giving help.' He distinguished his work from that of 'academic' psychology in that he was not interested in learning for its own sake but rather in helping people to develop in a healthy way.

Having detailed some of the strengths of Jung's approach to understanding adult personality development, let us now consider some of the weaknesses of Jungian theory.

The weaknesses of Jungian theory

Jung's theory of the individuation process in the second half of life was too closely tied to his own unique experience and to his personality type. Most people in our society do not have the time, education, or other resources to undergo the Jungian journey of individuation. To benefit fully from Jungian analysis, for example, one should be relatively affluent, well-read, and familiar with classical Greek mythology, articulate, and good at visualization of images, and have a relatively strong ego to be able to confront the instincts and images of the unconscious. In other words, Jung's procedure is designed particularly for a leisured, cultivated, creative elite.

Jungian analysis often tends towards solipsism and fails to deal with the question of personal relationships as the medium in which, ultimately, integration is achieved. In his writings on 'The psychology of the transference' (1970b), originally published in 1946, Jung indicated that individuation comes to fruition within the nurturing context of the analyst/patient relationship. Nevertheless, one sometimes gets the impression that Jung regarded individuation as an esoteric and largely internal process, the achievement of which takes place inside our own psyche. Finally, we must ask, if the Jungian path of healing entails a temporary withdrawal from the world in order to encounter the images of the unconscious, is there a path leading from individuation back to the world? Jung may not have seen this as a problem because he assumed that our relationship to the world is contained in our experience of the Self. On the other hand, for a Jungian like John Weir Perry (1974), individuation occurs as much in our activities in the world as in our dreams. The psyche is at work at all times and everywhere, not just in our dreams and fantasies.

Jung seems to have been relatively unaware of how important organizational worlds are in the lives of individuals in modern society. Adult personality development usually takes place in the context of work and family systems; it does not occur in a vacuum. Some recent Jungian theorists have acknowledged this (Fordham, 1957, 1958, 1978; Perry, 1974; Progoff, 1969; Singer, 1973), but the tendency in Jungian theory has been to emphasize the importance of the archetypal world of the unconscious to the relative exclusion of the social contexts in which we live. Jung had a keen sense of culture and history, but his understanding and interest in social structure, social institutions, and the web of social relationships was relatively underdeveloped as compared with his understanding of the inner world of the psyche. This lack in Jung's perspective probably derives from his introverted personality type. For Jung the subjectivity of his own experience was the fundamental reality, more valuable to him than any external events in his life, most of which he chose to exclude from his memoirs.

Jungian psychology can easily degenerate into an ersatz

religion in which the archetypes replace the gods and goddesses of earlier religious cults. Jung himself felt his mission
to be to offer a meaningful framework to people who had
lost their earlier religious beliefs. It is questionable whether
this is the proper task of psychology, viewed as a science.
On the other hand, it should be noted that Jung firmly
believed that he functioned as a scientist in his interpretation
of religious images. He firmly denied that he was or had any
intentions of being a religious leader. 'I have no message, no
mission; I attempt only to understand.' He spoke of himself
as a 'philosopher' in the sense of a lover of wisdom, thereby
attempting to 'avoid the sometimes questionable company of
those who offer a religion' (Jung, 1972c, p. 147). The
founder of a scientific theory or movement should not be
blamed for the activities, beliefs, and practices of his followers, and Jung is not to blame if his well-meaning disciples
have sometimes made a religion of analytical psychology
and a saint of its founder.

In Jung's work there is too much emphasis on archetypal
psychology and mythology and not enough attention to the
problems of individual development. Jung admitted that he
was not very interested in the personalia of people's lives;
he was much more interested in the collective, archetypal
level. In fact, he often farmed out his patients who had personal unconscious material to work through to his female
assistants to socialize them into the 'deeper' archetypal
journey of the soul (Hillman, 1976).

Jung's interpretation of development in the second half of
life is rather sketchy and abstract. It needs to be filled in
with a lot more detail regarding specific life tasks and patterns of development in late adulthood. Jung's principal
writings about adult development were composed during
the period of his middle adulthood, in his fifties. At that
time he was most interested in and knowledgeable about
mid-life; so it is understandable that his essays on development emphasize the importance of mid-life and the differences he noted between early and middle adulthood. What he
has to say about late adulthood, old age and death, we find

primarily in his memoirs, where his thoughts are presented unabashedly as his own personal reflections. He made no attempt to develop a systematic analysis of late adulthood.

I believe that as he grew older, Jung became less interested in the image of development or in correlating personality changes with stages in life. Instead he adopted the alchemical imagery of transformation of energy, a change that can take place at any point in the life cycle, and a process that continues throughout life. Furthermore, he came to see that all 'stages,' such as childhood, youth, maturity, and old age, exist simultaneously as archetypal structures in the psyche. The developmental model is more a reflection of the ego than the Self. The ego may develop in a linear trajectory, but with the Self there is only a circumambulation of the center, and a continuous unfolding out of the depths of the psyche.

One of the most telling critiques of Jung's developmental theory and technique came from one of his former students, Hans Trüb, who wrote in his book, *Heilung aus der Begegnung:*

> In our view Jung's achievement lies in the fact that he
> addressed himself in holy earnest to seek the self in the
> soul – and where else should he have sought it? – and that
> he pursued this hopeless path of inner enquiry to its very
> end . . . . In his endless endeavors to find man's self in
> the process of introversion, Jung accurately indicated the
> point of existential breakthrough. Although he himself
> did not succeed in breaking through from the ego to the
> Self, it was through his work that we now have been forced
> to realize that the breakthrough to universal reality can
> only come from this point, i.e., from the Self. In his
> investigation of the Collective Unconscious and in its
> therapeutic application Jung advanced as far as an intro-
> spective psychology can ever hope to advance, i.e., to the
> point where the psychic sphere, pointing beyond itself
> opens into the metaphysical (Trüb, 1962, p. 121).

Trüb objected to Jung's theory and practice on the grounds that the patient is only required to come to terms with the objects of his inner world, the archetypes, whilst his relationship to the outer world and to his fellow man is totally neglected. If Jung's path of healing and salvation achieves it fulfillment in 'individuation,' we may ask with Trüb, then is there a path leading from individuation back to the world? Trüb found Jung's answer unsatisfactory, when Jung told him that it was not necessary to seek a way back to the world because our relationship to the world is contained in our experience of the Self. Trüb concluded that the crucial deficiency in Jung's psychological theory of the individuation process and his archetypal psychology was that it was too closely tied to Jung's own particular personality structure. Jung was primarily a researcher and an introvert. He failed to prepare his patients for a new meeting with the world. He was so fascinated with the collective unconscious that he cut his own ties with the world and was thus incapable of guiding others back into the world after they made the symbolic quest under his tutelage as psychopomp.

In Jung's 'individuation process,' says Trüb, man's essential vocation is not so much developing his ability to contact, encounter, or adapt to his world, but rather to go inside and connect with his inner figures initiating a meeting between the conscious ego and other strata of the unconscious, a meeting which must take place before the Self can disclose itself and unfold as the emerging center of the personality. In short, Jung sees man's essential vocation in the psychological unfolding of his relationship with himself rather than in his relation to his world and to others. In Trüb's view, the Jungian hermetic circle is closed, restricting the individual's relationship to himself. It leaves out other persons and the wider world. The Thou or We is not embraced by individuation, says Trüb, influenced by Martin Buber, but only by the life of dialogue.[4] From this perspective, Jungian analysis appears to be a highly artificial situation rather like the generation of a baby in a test tube in which the psyche is only required to come to terms with itself in its quest for individuation and integration.

There is a Jungian answer to Trüb's critique, of course

Jung and the Jungians maintain that most of our behavior in the outer world is shaped, and perhaps even determined, by our own internal imagery. The necessary transformation of the personality can only come about through the careful observation and analysis of our inner imaginal world. Furthermore, in actual fact a discussion of one's external life patterns forms a significant part of any classical Jungian analysis, and attention to the client's adaptation to the outer world is a normal part of the analytic process.

It seems to me that the essence of most of the critiques of Jungian theory is that Jung's approach was too closely modeled on his own unique experience. Jung clearly set out to realize himself existentially through his own confrontation with the unconscious. He then went beyond this immediate aim by raising his own method of self-realization, which he called 'individuation,' to the status of a universal goal of healing, of salvation, and of the highest stage of human development. The other major criticism of Jung's theory is that it is elitist and not relevant to the majority of human beings who could never afford analysis. Jung was very clear that the individuation process was not for everybody, and he made no claim to its being a universal panacea for everyone. It requires more consciousness than most people are capable of. From Jung's point of view it seemed necessary and good that most people remained unconscious and devoted themselves to the tasks necessary to keep society running smoothly so that the chosen few who were 'called' by their daimones could individuate. Jung's model is Platonic, hierarchical, and elitist, not democratic.[5]

Strengths and limitations of contemporary adult development theory compared with Jung's approach

I now want to discuss the theorists mentioned earlier in Chapter 1, plus some recent theorists of adult development in relationship to Jung in order to assess what they have contributed to our understanding of adult development. My own opinion, stated repeatedly throughout this book is that Jung and ego developmental psychology complement each other. Both points of view are necessary for the formation of an adequate, comprehensive, holistic theory of development.

In Chapter 1, I discussed the early history of life-span, developmental psychology and the emergence of 'adulthood' as a specialized field of study. In my survey of current literature on 'adulthood' I discovered that the field is still in such an embryonic stage of development itself that there is not yet any fully developed theory currently available. The contributions of such pioneers as Bühler and Massarik (1968), Havinghurst (1948) and the socially oriented Chicago school, including Bernice Neugarten (1975) and her students, and the ego-developmental theories of Erikson (1950, 1968), Lovenger (1976), and the cognitive and moral developmental studies of Piaget (1965, 1975), and Kohlberg (1964, 1968, 1971), and the psychodynamic developmental theory of Nevitt Sanford (1966, 1973), have not yet been refined and integrated into a practical systems theory of adult developmental psychology.

The most comprehensive theory of adult development we have thus far is that of Levinson (1978) which was reviewed in detail in Chapter 1 of this dissertation. Levinson will probably expand the scope of his work in the coming years, but at the present time his work suffers from the drawback that his data base was limited to men and does not extend much beyond the mid-life transition and middle adulthood. Furthermore, his whole theory presupposes that adult development is correlated with ages and stages, and this is a hypothesis which still has not been demonstrated to hold true.

Current research in adult developmental psychology has tended to focus on rather narrow empirical studies of specific age-graded populations or on specific aspects of adult development such as the development of ego-strength and competence in adaptation to life (Lovenger, 1976; Vaillant, 1977), cognitive development (Gross, 1977), psychosexual development and identity (Erikson, 1950, 1968), or the development of aesthetic awareness (Read, 1963) and creativity in the later years (McLeish, 1976; Arieti, 1976). While these studies are valuable additions to our knowledge about adulthood, none of them manage to take the broader, more holistic view which I have advocated and which I believe Jung embodied and exemplified.

One of the main problems of contemporary adult developmental psychology is that it has tended to place primary emphasis on 'normal' patterns of development (Sheehy, 1976) without sufficient attention to 'abnormal' or 'subnormal' patterns. What is viewed as 'normal' in one culture may be seen as 'abnormal' in another and vice versa. Furthermore, schizophrenia and psychoses may be viewed as appropriate responses to life tasks which appear to be overwhelmingly demanding to the individual who retreats into childhood and infantile states (Laing, 1970; Perry, 1974). It seems to me that studies of these extreme and pathological modes of adaptation, such as Jung's study of Miss Miller's fantasies in his book *Symbols of Transformation* illuminate the larger archetypal framework in which all individual development occurs. Probably what the study of psychoses adds more than anything else to current adult developmental psychology is an awareness of the importance of the unconscious in guiding and impeding the developmental processes currently receiving attention.

The main thrust of non-Jungian adult developmental psychology has been to emphasize ego mastery and adaptation to life. It may be no accident that some of the principal studies of adult development have been designed by males to study male adult development in American society. In American culture the emphasis on ego mastery is very much of a male attitude, although this may be changing. One might also say that most adult developmental psychology has been created by and for extraverts, for whom the external world is the primary reality. It is only to be expected that extraverts tend to underestimate the significance of the individual and collective psyche in their lives which are usually focused primarily on adaptation to external rather than to internal conditions.

Throughout this work I have argued that Jung's intro-verted Self-psychology complements and supplements mainstream adult developmental psychology. It is not surpris-ing that in his book *Psychological Types* (1971), Jung empha-sized the difference and complementarity between those who adapt more easily to the outer world or to the inner world. Being constituted as he was, Jung saw the world differently from extraverted psychologists. He never claimed that his theory had all the answers, but he did believe that it comple-mented the prevailing extraverted orientation of scientific psychology as he knew it. He liked to say that he offered the point of view from the other side of the moon, by which he meant from the other side of ego consciousness, i.e., from the objective psyche, or collective unconscious. While the goal of Jungian therapy is balance and wholeness, the individua-tion process may be viewed as a kind of socialization to introversion, an education of the soul to complement the extraverted style of our formal schooling and of our culture at large.

In contrast to most other developmental psychologists, Jung and his followers emphasized the impersonal universal structures of the psyche expressed in dreams, myths, and creative products more than ego-development and mastery. Through the use of comparative material drawn from other epochs and cultures than our own, Jung was able to amplify and give a larger context for the products of the creative psyche than personal biography, or psychoanalysis, or even psychodynamic ego psychology could give.

If we take Jung's theory seriously we can no longer go along with the narrow emphasis of most developmental psychology on the achievement of ego goals and mastery of the environment. Instead, we will begin to value equally the more 'feminine' intuitive energy of introversion, and we will measure personality development in terms of the balance of the whole personality.

I believe that the adult developmental psychology of the

future will combine the virtues of both ego-psychology and Jung's Self-psychology, in a broader holistic systems perspective. Perhaps the foundations for this new synthesis may be found in the new psychology of consciousness (Ornstein, 1973). For example, the extravert/introvert dichotomy may be a reflection of our bimodal brain structure, the left brain being analytical and rational and the right brain being synthetic and intuitive. From this perspective Jung may be viewed as a bridge figure between both the neo-Freudian and ego-developmental theories of Erikson, Levinson, and Sanford, on the one hand, and the emerging new systems-oriented psychology of consciousness, on the other.

Beyond adult development

I believe that we need a broader, more comprehensive, holistic synoptic framework and conception of human development than is now available. Although I do not feel ready to articulate such a theory in depth, I can indicate what I believe are the conditions necessary for such a theory, and the attitudes I believe that the future holistic developmentalist should hold towards the field.

Multidimensional. The holistic developmentalist will take a multidimensional view of the whole person, considering the development of the physical, emotional, rational, and intuitive dimensions of the person. These categories parallel Jung's sensation, feeling, thinking, and intuitive functions and the psycho-motor, affective, and cognitive functions considered in contemporary educational psychology. I agree with Jung that development occurs in several different areas of the self, each of which may be more or less developed, and that the goal of human development is balance or wholeness, based on the unique combination of hereditary, environmental, and existential factors in each person's life. Such a multidimensional theory will also consider human energy levels and energy transformation as an aspect of developmental change.

From this perspective the bodymind is viewed as a holistic unity or interacting system, and diagnosis of illness entails evaluation of the total state of the bodymind. The holistic developmentalist will interpret the flow of psychic energy in terms of the coincidence of opposites and will incorporate a variety of models, Oriental and Western, for the dynamic development of the psyche.

Dialectical.   A dialectical developmentalist will observe the interplay between the ego and non-ego aspects of the self, including the archetypal and transpersonal dimensions. In particular, he will look for and nurture the emergence of what Jung called the 'transcendent function,' or 'transpersonal control point' beyond the dialectical play of opposites in the psyche. Such a dialectical theory also 'focuses on and tries to overcome the separation of organism and environment, consciousness and behavior, subject and object (Riegel, 1978, p. 9). The dialectical developmentalist 'incorporates divergent viewpoints and integrates them at higher and more inclusive levels' (Riegel, 1978, p. 9). (Dialectical psychology and sociology, like dialectical philosophy, are foreign to the Anglo-American empiricist tradition, but dialectics lie at the foundation of the European intellectual tradition and can be traced back to Plato, who viewed dialectic as 'the ability to see the connections of things,' Plato, *The Republic*, 533c.)

Integrative.   A holistically oriented developmentalist actively works toward the integration of the personality while noting its differentiation and complexity. He views development as a movement from simplicity to ever increasing complexity, as a series of transitions involving integration of an ever wider variety of viewpoints, ideas, perspectives, and sensibilities in the self. I believe that integration of the personality can never be completed because development entails a dialectical process in which every synthesis eventually breaks up (or down) in the course of life then offering the possibility of a new higher level of integration.

Interdisciplinary.   Drawing upon biology, sociology, psychology, anthropology, history, the humanities, and other disciplines, the holistic developmentalist recognizes that human development is complex and multidimensional, and requires the perspectives of specialists from many different disciplines. Take for example the study of lives such as the life of C. G. Jung. An adequate interpretation of the adult development of a person like Jung requires a familiarity with social and intellectual history, religion, philosophy, psychology, sociology, anthropology, art and literature, philosophical biology, modern physics, and human development.

Ecological, systems-oriented.   The holistic developmentalist recognizes that individuals develop in socio-cultural contexts and different geographic and natural settings. He will consider whether and how these environments nurture or stifle development. He knows that the same laws govern the evolution and development of all living systems from amino acids to organizations and macroeconomic systems.

Political and sociological.   He will consider the role of power, conflict, social structures, and institutions as one of the principle dimensions and domains within which human beings develop (or fail to do so).

Religious.   He will recognize that man is a religious animal and that philosophy, religion, mythology, and theology stimulate and motivate man's dreams and actions and provide the guiding images of both their personal and their cultural development.

Aesthetic and symbolically oriented.   Such a theory will take into account the importance of symbols and images and works of art and music in the development of human consciousness and culture.

Comparative and cross-cultural.   The holistic developmentalist knows that any generalizations he makes about human development must be tested to discover the extent to which they are culture-bound or actually universal. He recognizes that most current writing on adult development in the United States today is really American ethnography like most American sociology. Jung took great pains to test his generalizations and conclusions through careful comparative studies. Contemporary adult developmental psychologists could do well to follow Jung's example in this regard.

Practical.   If a theory is any good, it will be usable in practice and will lead to guidelines for action. Too often research in human development and aging seems to be mere data-gathering with little theoretical reflection or practical implications. Holistic developmentalists will be interested in developing a practical theory designed to assist people in coming to terms with the aging process.[6]

We do not yet have an adequate conceptual framework for a holistic approach to human development and aging. We have no single theory to understand the various aspects of the human condition in relation to health or development. There are certain models and techniques, however, such as the Freudian, Jungian, behavioristic, humanistic and transpersonal psychologies, that can deal successfully with some aspects of development in different individuals and cultures.

What I advocate, therefore, in the present situation in which there is a mosaic of models, is a 'bootstrap' approach similar to the one used in contemporary physics. We must continue to develop a mosaic of models of limited scope that are mutually consistent. It will be the role of the developmentalist, therapist, or educator to find out which model or approach is most suitable for a particular client or situation.

As we develop a holistic theory of adult development and move beyond the Freudian and behavioristic, deterministic worldviews, we will be able to appreciate Jung's work more and he may begin to influence future adult development theory.

Epilogue

The old man sat at his desk, prowling through dusty old books and his own hand-written commentaries and manuscripts. Some people who knew him said that he often hummed and muttered to himself while he worked. The room in which he worked was large. The walls were filled with books. A window looked out of the tower on to the lake. Outside he could hear the waterfowl sing, chatter, and quack. No one was allowed to disturb him while he worked. He was determined to complete this one last book before he departed this life. It was to be the revelation of the ultimate secrets of alchemy, and indirectly of the human soul.

What are we to make of this wise old man today? He was one who pushed on fearlessly into those realms of the mind and soul where most of us dare not go. Yet many have been there before. The ancient Egyptians and the wise old Tibetans knew this realm well. It is depicted in their Books of the Dead. The early Christian Gnostics knew it from personal experience as well, though their descriptions of this experience are mostly lost to us. We know of their spiritual adventures largely from the accounts of their adversaries, never the best source, especially of inner experience. The alchemists were linked by a Golden Chain to these earlier traditions, but many others have explored these realms independently, Often they were living in institutions of one kind or another, monasteries or mental hospitals. Sometimes they managed to contact this frightening yet wondrous inner world and yet to be able to cope, to live in the world 'outside', a world where 'they' – the spirits – remained largely unknown.

Lacking an adequately supportive and confirming refer- ence group of males among his own contemporaries, Jung surrounded himself with a group of intelligent and admiring female disciples in Zurich who have carried on the Jungian tradition since his death. The Zurich *Jungfrauen*, who some- times jokingly referred to themselves as his Manaeds, included Drs Jolande Jacoby, Marie-Louise von Franz, Aniela Jaffé, and Mrs Barbara Hannah. More important to him than all of these, of course, was his beloved Antonia Wolff, who he liked to think of as his 'anima,' and 'soror mystica.'

For a male reference group he turned to the past, to the ancient Egyptian Gnostics, to the mystics, magicians, human- ists, and alchemists of the sixteenth and seventeenth cen- turies, to Goethe and to his renowned grandfather Carl Gustav Jung, who had reorganized the Faculty of Medicine at Basel University in the early nineteenth century.

At the end of his life, Jung isolated himself – voluntarily – in his tower study in Bollingen. Reading his memoirs, one gets the impression that he felt isolated during much of his life; however, the facts reported by people who knew him belie this story. Perhaps unconsciously Jung felt a need to be isolated, but did not like to acknowledge this. By the end of his life he had accommodated himself to his 'fate,' and had learned to enjoy his solitude knowing it to be the fertile ground of his own creativity.

It is a difficult and lonely life to be a visionary, an artist, a seer, a mystic. Carl Gustav Jung was such a person. Yet by the end of his life, he had learned to live with his loneliness. He not only accepted it with resignation, as his inescapable lot, he often savoured it. For he knew that it was the source of his creativity. Even as a child, he felt himself to be alone. He was alone throughout most of his life, as must be anyone who knows things that others do not know, who sees things and hears voices that are not known by others, by those sensible people who live in the 'world', those denizens of the flatland.

Jung had his 'secret,' his premonition of things unknown. His life had meaning to him because behind his personal life he knew there was something impersonal, a *numinosum*, as he called it. His writings, even his memoirs, reflect his belief in the singularity and importance of his experience, of the impersonal dimension in his life as being its essence. Jung took it for granted that the unexpected and the incredible belong in this world. For him the world always seemed to be infinite and ungraspable. He was temperamentally attuned to those background vibrations and processes that are generally not so evident to those more conventional people we call sane. In fact, some of his readers have judged Jung as being a near psychotic or schizophrenic person. The borderline between mysticism and madness has always been a thin one. Jung lived on the border, challenging and questioning those easy truths most of us take for granted as part of our assumptive world.

Naturally, Jung had trouble getting his ideas accepted. Much of what he said flew in the face of 'common sense,' of what his contemporaries 'knew' to be the case. But Jung 'knew' his own truths. As his life neared its end, he decided, after much inner questioning, to set down his recollections of his inner experience, to tell his own personal myth.

The story I have told is a tale of a person who very early in his life discovered that he was two. It is the story of the relationship, of Carl Gustav Jung and his 'other self,' his second personality, his daimon. I see and sense a deep underlying continuity running through the whole of C.G. Jung's long life. This continuity is not to be found so much in his theories, as in his fundamental character structure and in his unceasing attempts to learn to live with and understand his split nature. I believe that it was a result of his own dual character, and his inability ever to fully heal or transcend his inner divisions, that led him to identify very early in his youth with the Faust story, as told by Goethe. It may be that in the act of writing his memoirs shortly before his death in his eighty-sixth year the 'wise old man from Küsnacht' did finally attain to a 'unit self,' an integrated totality, to that wholeness of personality that he so often spoke of as an ideal in his writings. My intention in this book has not been so much to tell of Jung's achievements, as to understand his inner dynamics and to place him and his life story in a social-historical and cultural context. Whether Jung or his followers acknowledged it or not, he was definitely working within a particular intellectual and cultural tradition, the German romantic, idealist, religious and philosophical tradition.[1]

In his *Memories, Dreams and Reflections*, Carl Gustav Jung recollected the story of his inner life, of his dreams and visions, of his relationships and of his travels. In this book he presented his life as a story of the self-realization of the unconscious. From his point of view, the only events in his life that were 'worth telling' were 'those when the imperishable world irrupted into this transitory one.' His dreams and visions formed the *prima materia* for his scientific work. All other memories of events, people, and his surroundings paled by comparison with these interior happenings. He thought of his life, of all life, in fact, as being like a plant that lives on its rhizome. Its true life is invisible. The part that appears above ground lasts only a short time, then it withers away.

> When we think of the unending growth and decay of life and civilizations, we cannot escape the impression of absolute nullity. Yet I have never lost a sense of something that lives and endures underneath the eternal flux. What we see is the blossom which passes. The rhizome remains (Jung, 1961).

If there was any direction in his long life, old C. G. Jung concluded, it lay in the gradual unfolding of his inner potentialities, of the contents of his unconscious spurred on by the daimon of creativity. Like one of his heroes, Dr Faustus, Jung had felt himself driven by his daimon. 'I could never stop at anything once attained. I had to hasten on, to catch up with my vision.' At the same time, he trusted his inner promptings for, as he said, 'I know that I exist on the foundation of something I do not know. In spite of all uncertainties, I feel a solidity underlying all existence and a continuity in my mode of being.'

Speaking of his autobiography, and of his fears that what he wrote in it would be misunderstood, he said:

> I have guarded this material all my life and have never wanted it exposed to the world; for if it is assailed, I shall be affected even more than in the case of my other books. I do not know whether I shall be so far removed from this world that the arrows of criticism will no longer reach me and that I shall be able to bear the adverse reactions. I have suffered enough from incomprehension and from the isolation one falls into when one says things that people do not understand. If the Job book met with so much misunderstanding, my 'memoirs' will have an even more unfortunate fate. The 'autobiography' is my life, viewed in the light of the knowledge I have gained from my scientific endeavors. Both are one, and therefore this book makes great demands on people who do not know or cannot understand my scientific ideas. My life has been in a sense the quintessence of what I have written, not the other way around. The way I am and the way I write are a unity. All my ideas and all my endeavors are myself. Thus the 'autobiography' is merely the dot on the i.
>
> If I ask the value of my life, I can only measure myself against the centuries and then I must say, Yes, it does mean something. [But] measured by the ideas of today, it means nothing (Jung, 1961, p. vi).

The *Collected Works* might equally well be entitled 'The making of C. G. Jung.' It is not so much an *opus scientificum* – for given the subject, it could never be that – as it is a large and complex metaphor for all that he knew about the process of becoming a Self – i.e., his unique Self, a heritage and an experience.

In my view Jung's work was more mythic than scientific. His was a representative and symbolic life, and his works were his theoretical reflection on that lived experience. It isn't that Jung was less than a scientist, he was more. He was a man who led a very full and rich life and who, in his works and writings, created metaphors to express his experience.

> The long path I have traversed is littered with husks sloughed off, witnesses to countless moultings, these relicta one calls books. They conceal as much as they reveal. Every step is a symbol of those to follow. He who mounts a flight of steps does not linger on them, even though age invites him to linger or slow down his pace . . . . The last steps are the loveliest and most precious, for they lead to that fullness to which the innermost essence of man is born (Jung, 1973b).

Notes

Preface
1 Recent interpretations of adult development include: Erik Erikson, (ed.) *Adulthood.* New York: Daedalus Books, 1978. Roger Gould, *Transformations. Growth and Change in Adult Life.* New York: Simon & Schuster, 1978.
2 See my essay on Freud, Jung and Lévi-Strauss in *Theory and Society*, 3 (1976) and Ira Progoff's fine book *Jung's Psychology and its Social Meaning.*

Chapter 1 The emergence of adult development psychology
1 Jung's discussion of adult developmental psychology is scattered throughout his writings, but the essence of his theory can be found in his essays 'The stages of life.' in the *Collected Works*, vol. 8 and 'The development of personality' in the *Collected Works*, vol. 17.

Chapter 2 The making of a scientist
1 Dr Alphonse Maeder, who was on the Burgholzli staff at the same time as Jung, reported in a personal communication to Henry Ellenberger that at the Burgholzli

> the patient was the focus of interest. The student learned how to talk with him. Burgholzli was at that time a kind of factory where you worked very much and were poorly paid. Everyone from the professor to the young resident was totally absorbed by his work. Abstinence from alcoholic drinks was imposed on everyone. Bleuler was kind to all and never played the role of the chief (Ellengerger, 1970, p. 667).

2 Jung seems to have looked upon the voice of the Devil as synonymous with his No. 1 personality, and the voice of God with his No. 2. He seems to imply that the ego is the enemy that must be suppressed, and in fact he did maintain that every manifestation of

the Self is a defeat for the ego. Such a Manichean view of the psyche is highly dramatic, but not necessarily true. Hillman's critique of Jung's crypto-monotheism provides a healthy alternative perspective. In his view the Self is simply another complex among others, not the superordinate central archetype that Jung makes it out to be. Cf. James Hillman, 'Psychology: monotheistic or polytheistic?' *Spring*, 1971, pp. 193–208 and *Re-Visioning Psychology*. New York: Harper & Row, 1975.

3 Homans (1979) interpreted Jung's relationship with Freud in terms of Kohut's theory of narcissism. He shows how during his psycho-analytic years Jung 'developed a narcissistic merger with Freud.' The disintegration of this relationship left Jung with an acute sense of narcissistic injury and vulnerability. His needs for esteem and his potential for grandiosity, formerly available in his relationship with Freud, were now frustrated.

> By constructing the theory of archetypes and all that goes with it -- he interposed interpretive categories between his own mind and these cultural products thereby separating himself from them. By naming his inner experiences, he created his system of psychological ideas. In so doing he achieved both personal, psychological distance from himself and his merger with the cultural products of the past and also a new interpretive theory that could be applied to the past. (p. 83)

4 Homans observed that Jung's confrontation with the unconscious centered upon the three most important relations in human life: a guiding male figure or mentor, a female figure, and representations of the pure self. 'It is not surprising,' he comments, 'that the heart of the individuation process should consist of an encounter between the conscious ego and the archetypes of the mother, the father, and the self' (p. 83). Jung believed that the images he encountered in the unconscious were 'other' than himself. For him they were universal, archetypal primordial images, not personal and individualistic, as he would have interpreted them had he remained within the Freudian system. Homans, on the other hand, maintains that although these images could not be adequately interpreted in terms of Freud's theory of the repression of sexual fantasies, they did have a basis in personal experience, and can be understood as preoedipal and narcissistic tendencies in Jung's personal organization.

Chapter 3   Jung's mid-life transition
1 This painting appears as Figure 3 in 'The secret of the golden flower,' in *Alchemical studies*, the *Collected Works*, vol. 13, 1967.

Chapter 4 The development of Jung's theory of the individuation process in the second half of life

1 Colin Wilson gives an alternative interpretation of this case in his book *New Pathways in Psychology. Maslow and the Post-Freudian Revolution.* London: Gollancz, 1972.

2 Remember that in Jung's view the meaning and purpose of the second half of life was 'culture,' just as 'nature' was the priority of the first half.

Chapter 5 Conclusion

1 Jung never tired of insisting that he was, first and last, a medical man and an empiricist, not a philosopher or theorist. 'I am not a philosopher. I am not a sociologist – I am a medical man. I deal with facts. This cannot be emphasized too much.' He insisted that he was 'an empiricist who discovers certain facts and erects hypotheses to explain them, but who is not responsible for the implications, philosophical or otherwise, that may be drawn from his statements.' He complained that he was often accused of making philosophical statements because he made use of *philosophical concepts*, and because he did not shy away from making his assumptions clear. 'I am not particularly well read in philosophy,' he said. 'I simply have had to make use of philosophical concepts to formulate my findings.' What first attracted him to Freud, he said, was that 'he was not much of a philosopher, he was strictly a medical man. I had read these philosophers [Kant, Schopenhauer, C.G. Carus, and Eduard von Hartmann] long before I ever saw Freud. I came to Freud for *facts*.' Statements of Jung from his interview with Ximena de Angulo published in *C.G. Jung Speaking. Interviews and Encounters*, edited by William McGuire and R.F.C. Hull (Princeton, Princeton University Press, Bollingen Series XCVII, 1977), pp. 206–8.

2 From the beginning of his intellectual life, Jung had been fascinated with comparative zoology.

> 'I was especially interested in palaeontology; you see, my life work in historical comparative psychology is like palaeontology. That is the study of the archetypes of the animals, and this is the study of the archetypes in the soul. The Eohippus is the archetype of the modern horse, the archetypes are like the fossil animals.' (ibid., p. 209)

3 Although Jung did not have a direct influence upon the development of organismic theory and self-actualization theory in psychology, in their textbook on *Theories of Personality* Calvin S. Hall and Gardner Lindzey praise Jung as a forerunner and indirect influence on

Goldstein, Rogers, Angyl, Allport, and Maslow. Hall and Lindzey acknowledge that 'in no instance do we find Jung being credited with the development of this conception. This in itself does not mean that Jung has had no influence, whether directly or indirectly, upon these men' (1970, p. 111). The main difference between Jung and the organismic theorists was his emphasis on the unconscious.

4   Buber (1952) criticized Jung for being a 'modern Gnostic' who 'oversteps with sovereign license the boundaries of psychology' and ends in solipsism. Buber maintained in contrast to Jung, that 'my soul does not and cannot include the other, and yet can nonetheless approach the other in real contact.' The other is a 'Thou,' over against my 'I'. 'All beings existing over against me who become "included" in my self are possessed by it in this inclusion as an It.' Buber rejected Jung's psychic imperialism. Only when we recognize the 'unincludable otherness of a being' and renounce all claim to 'incorporating' it into our own souls does it truly become Thou for us. This holds good for God as well as for man. The result is 'a genuine contact with the existing being who meets me, to full and direct reciprocity with him. It leads from the soul which places reality in itself to the soul which enters reality' (p. 89).

5   Homans (1979) criticizes Jung's deep suspicion of the social order as a source for authentic living: 'the force of the Jungian system on the whole moves against the social order and commends a self that is free from its compelling influence and power' (p. 200).

> In all this, Jung rendered normative a lack of meaning in the public sphere. He spoke against the institutional structuring of the personal sector of life, creating in effect a doctrine of the private self. All the social, political, and religious structures that formerly existed apart from the individual self were re-interpreted as psychological processes. . . . Freud's cultural superego, the political structures of mass society and the state, and the mystery of God's transcendent reality were all rendered into psychological form. In the world of Jung's thought, the mind became society and church – a world within a world. (pp. 200–1)

6   The beginnings of a practical holistic approach to adult development and aging may be seen in Gay Luce's *Your Second Life. Vitality and Growth in Middle and Later Years* (1979) and in John-Raphael Staude (ed.) *Wisdom and Age* (1981).

Epilogue
1   In *The Discovery of the Unconscious, The History and Evolution of Dynamic Psychiatry* (New York, Basic Books, 1970), Henri F. Ellenberger indicated many parallels between Freudian and Jungian concepts and the basic ideas of German romanticism and idealism.

Bibliography

Arieti, S. (1976), *Creativity. The Magic Synthesis*. New York: Basic Books.

Baltes, P., and Schaie, K. W. (eds) (1973), *Life-Span Developmental Psychology. Personality and Socialization*. New York: Academic Press.

Binswanger, L. (1957), *Sigmund Freud. Reminiscences of a Friendship*, N. Guterman (trans.). New York: Grune & Stratton.

Brome, V. (1978), *Jung*. New York: Atheneum.

Buber, M. (1952), *Eclipse of God*. New York: Harper & Row.

Bugental, J. F. T. (1976), *The Search for Existential Identity*. San Francisco: Jossey-Bass.

Bühler, C. and Massarik, F. (eds) (1968), *The Course of Human Life*. New York: Springer.

Capra, F. (1975), *The Tao of Physics*. Berkeley: Shambala.

Ellenberger, H. (1970), *The Discovery of the Unconscious. The History and Evolution of Dynamic Psychiatry*. New York: Basic Books.

Erikson, E. H. (1950), *Childhood and Society*. New York: Norton.

Erikson, E. H. (1958), *Young Man Luther*. New York: Norton.

Erikson, E. H. (1968), *Identity, Youth and Crisis*. New York: Norton.

Erikson, E. H. (1969), *Gandhi's Truth. On the Origins of Militant Nonviolence*. New York: Norton.

Fordham, M. (1957), *New Developments in Analytical Psychology*. London: Routledge & Kegan Paul.

Fordham, M. (1958), *The Objective Psyche*. London: Routledge & Kegan Paul.

Fordham, M. (1978), *Jungian Psychotherapy. A Study in Analytical Psychology*. New York: Wiley.

Frankl, V. (1966), *Man's Search for Meaning: An Introduction to Logotherapy*. I. Lasch (trans.) New York: Washington Square.

Freud, S. (1917), 'On narcissism: an introduction'. In *Complete Psychological Works* (ed. J. Strachey). London: The Hogarth Press.

Fromm, E. (1951), *The Forgotten Language*. New York: Grove.

Giner, S. (1976), *Mass Society*. New York: Academic Press.

Goldstein, K. (1939), *The Organism*. New York: American Book Co.

Gross, R. (1977), *The Lifelong Learner*. New York: Simon & Schuster.

Hall, G. S. (1904), *Adolescence* (2 vols). New York: Appleton Century Crofts.

Hall, G. S. (1922), *Senescence: The Last Half of Life*. New York: Appleton Century Crofts.

Hall, C. S. and Lindzey, G. (1970), *Theories of Personality*. New York: Wiley.

Havinghurst, R. J. (1948), *Developmental Tasks and Education*. New York: David McKay.

Havinghurst, R. J. (1973), 'History of developmental psychology.' In P. Baltes and K. W. Schaie (eds), *Life-Span Developmental Psychology. Personality and Socialization*, New York: Academic Press.

Hegel, G. F. W. (1967), *The Phenomenology of the Mind*, J. Baille (trans.) New York: Harper & Row.

Hillman, J. (1975), *Re-Visioning Psychology*. New York: Harper & Row.

Hillman, J. (1976), 'Puer/Senex.' In *Eranos Yearbook*, vol. 36. Leiden: Brill.

Hillman, J. (1976), Personal communication.

Homans, P. (1979), *Jung in Context. Modernity and the Making of a Psychology*. Chicago: University of Chicago Press.

Horney, K. (1950), *Neurosis and Human Growth*. New York: Norton.

Jacques, E. (1970), *Work, Creativity and Social Justice*. New York: International Universities Press.

Jones, E. (1955), *Sigmund Freud. Life and Work*, vol. 2: *Years of Maturity 1901-1919*. London: Hogarth Press.

Jung, C. G. (1925), 'Notes on the Seminar on Analytical Psychology'. Zurich: March 23 to July 6, 1925.

Jung, C. G. (1958), 'Transformation symbolism in the mass.' In H. Read, M. Fordham, G. Adler, and W. McGuire (eds), R. F. C. Hull (trans.), *Psychology and Religion: West and East* (vol. 11 of the *Collected Works*, Bollingen Series, XX). Princeton University Press; London: Routledge & Kegan Paul.

Jung, C. G. (1961), *Memories, Dreams and Reflections*. A. Jaffe (recorded and ed.). R. Winston and C. Winston (trans.). New York: Pantheon Books.

Jung, C. G. (1964a), 'The development of personality.' In H. Read, M. Fordham, G. Adler, and W. McGuire (eds), R. F. C. Hull (trans.), *The Development of Personality* (vol. 17 of the *Collected Works*, Bollingen Series, XX). Princeton University Press; London: Routledge & Kegan Paul.

Jung, C. G. (1964b), 'Marriage as a psychological relationship.' In H. Read, M. Fordham, G. Adler, and W. McGuire (eds), R. F. C. Hull (trans.), *The Development of Personality* (vol. 17 of the *Collected Works*, Bollingen Series, XX). Princeton University Press; London: Routledge & Kegan Paul.

Jung, C. G. (1964c), 'Analytical psychology and education.' In H. Read, M. Fordham, G. Adler, and W. McGuire (eds), R. F. C. Hull (trans.), *The Development of Personality*, (vol. 17 of the *Collected Works*, Bollingen Series, XX). Princeton University Press; London: Routledge & Kegan Paul.

Jung, C. G. (1966a), 'The ego and the unconscious.' In H. Read, M. Fordham, G. Adler, and W. McGuire (eds), R. F. C. Hull (trans.), *Two Essays in Analytical Psychology* (2nd edn), (vol. 7 of the *Collected Works*, Bollingen Series, XX). Princeton University Press; London: Routledge & Kegan Paul.

Jung, C. G. (1966b), *Two Essays in Analytical Psychology* (2nd edn). H. Read, M. Fordham, G. Adler, and W. McGuire (eds), R. F. C. Hull (trans.), (vol. 7 of the *Collected Works*, Bollingen Series, XX). Princeton University Press; London: Routledge & Kegan Paul.

Jung, C. G. (1967a), *Symbols of Transformation* (2nd edn). H. Read, M. Fordham, G. Adler, and W. McGuire (eds), R. F. C. Hull (trans.), (vol. 5 of the *Collected Works*, Bollingen Series, XX). Princeton University Press; London: Routledge & Kegan Paul.

Jung, C. G. (1967b), *Septem Sermones ad Mortuos.* London: Stuart & Watkins.

Jung, C. G. (1967c), 'The secret of the golden flower.' In H. Read, M. Fordham, G. Adler, and W. McGuire (eds), R. F. C. Hull (trans.), *Alchemical Studies*, (vol. 13 of the *Collected Works*, Bollingen Series, XX). Princeton University Press; London: Routledge & Kegan Paul.

Jung, C. G. (1970a), 'The psychology and pathology of so-called occult phenomena.' In H. Read,. M. Fordham, G. Adler, and W. McGuire (eds), R. F. C. Hull (trans.), *Psychiatric Studies* (2nd edn), (vol. 1 of the *Collected Works*, Bollingen Series, XX). Princeton University Press; London: Routledge & Kegan Paul.

Jung, C. G. (1970b), 'The psychology of the transference.' In H. Read, M. Fordham, G. Adler, and W. McGuire (eds), R. F. C. Hull (trans.), *The Practice of Psychotherapy*, (vol. 16 of the *Collected Works*, Bollingen Series, XX). Princeton University Press; London: Routledge & Kegan Paul.

Jung, C. G. (1971). *Psychological Types.* In H. Read, M. Fordham, G. Adler, and W. McGuire (eds), R. F. C. Hull (trans.), (vol. 6 of the *Collected Works*, Bollingen Series, XX). Princeton University Press; London: Routledge & Kegan Paul.

Jung, C. G. (1972a), 'The stages of life.' In H. Read, M. Fordham, G. Adler, and W. McGuire (eds), R. F. C. Hull (trans.), *The Structure and Dynamics of the Psyche* (2nd edn), (vol. 8 of the *Collected*

Works, Bollingen Series, XX). Princeton University Press; London: Routledge & Kegan Paul.

Jung, C. G. (1972b), 'The transcendent function.' In H. Read, M. Fordham, G. Adler, and W. McGuire (eds), R. F. C. Hull (trans.), *The Structure and Dynamics of the Psyche* (2nd edn), (vol. 8 of the *Collected Works,* Bollingen Series, XX). Princeton University Press; London: Routledge & Kegan Paul.

Jung, C. G. (1972c), 'Is analytical psychology a religion?' *Spring,* pp. 144-9.

Jung, C. G. (1973a), 'Diagnostic association studies.' In H. Read, M. Fordham, G. Adler, and W. McGuire (eds), R. F. C. Hull (trans.), *Experimental Researches,* (vol. 2 of the *Collected Works,* Bollingen Series, XX). Princeton University Press; London: Routledge & Kegan Paul.

Jung, C. G. (1973b), *Letters.* Princeton University Press.

Jung, C. G. (1974), *Aion. Researches into the Phenomenology of the Self* (2nd edn). H. Read, M. Fordham, G. Adler, and W. McGuire (eds), R. F. C. Hull (trans.), (vol. 9, Part 2 of the *Collected Works,* Bollingen Series, XX). Princeton University Press; London: Routledge & Kegan Paul.

Jung, C. G. (1977), 'The symbolic life.' H. Read, M. Fordham, G. Adler, and W. McGuire (eds), R. F. C. Hull (trans.), (vol. 18 of the *Collected Works,* Bollingen Series, XX). Princeton University Press; London: Routledge & Kegan Paul.

Koestenbaum, P. (1978), *The New Image of the Person.* Westport, Conn.: Greenwood Press.

Kohlberg, L. (1964), 'Development of moral character and moral ideology.' *Review of Child Development Research,* vol. 1. New York: Russell Sage Foundation.

Kohlberg, L. (1968), 'Moral development.' *International Encyclopedia of Social Sciences.* New York: Macmillan Free Press.

Kohlberg, L. (1971), 'Cognitive-development theory and the practice of collective moral education.' In M. Wollins and M. Gottesman (eds), *Group Care: the Education Path of Youth Aliyah.* New York: Gordon & Breach.

Kohut, H. (1977), *The Restoration of the Self.* New York: International Universities Press.

Laing, R. (1970). *The Politics of Experience.* New York: Bantam.

Levinson, D. (1980), 'Explorations in Biography.' In *Further Explorations in Personality.* New York: Wiley.

Levinson, D., Darrow, C. N. Klein, E. B., Levinson, M. H., and McKee, B. (1978), *The Seasons of a Man's Life.* New York: Knopf.

Lovenger, J. (1976), *Ego Development.* San Francisco: Jossey-Bass.

Luce, G. (1979), *Your Second Life. Vitality and Growth in Middle and Later Years.* New York: Delacorte Press/Seymour Lawrence.

Luft, D. (1980), *Robert Musil and the Crisis of European Culture (1880-1942)*. Berkeley and Los Angeles: University of California Press.

McGuire, W. (ed.) (1974), *The Freud/Jung Letters*, R. Manheim and R. F. C. Hull (trans). London: The Hogarth Press and Routledge & Kegan Paul.

McLeish, J. A. B. (1976), *The Ulyssean Adult. Creativity in the Middle and Later Years*. New York:McGraw Hill.

Mann, T. (1957), *Essays*. New York: Random House.

Maslow, A. H. (1954), *Towards a Psychology of Being*. New York: Van Nostrand Rineholt.

Maslow, A. H. (1968), *Towards a Psychology of Being* (2nd edn). New York: Van Nostrand Rineholt.

Maslow, A. H. (1970), *Motivation and Personality* (2nd edn). New York: Harper & Row.

Maslow, A. H. (1971), *The Further Reaches of Human Nature*. New York: Viking Press.

May, R. (1976), *The Courage to Create*. New York: Bantam.

Mayer, N. (1978), *The Male Mid-Life Crisis*. New York: Doubleday.

Murray, H. A. (1962), *Carl Gustav Jung. 1875-1961. A Memorial Meeting*. New York: The Analytical Psychology Club of New York.

Neugarten, B. (ed.) (1975), *Middle Age and Aging*. University of Chicago Press.

Norton, D. L. (1976), *Personal Destinies. A Philosophy of Ethical Individualism*. Princeton University Press.

Ogilvy, J. (1977), *Many Dimensional Man. Decentralizing Self, Society, and the Sacred*. New York: Oxford University Press.

Olney, J. (1980), *The Rhizome and the Flower. The Perennial Philosophy - Yeats and Jung*. Berkeley and Los Angeles: University of California Press.

Ornstein, R. (1973), *On the Psychology of Consciousness*. New York: Viking Press.

Perry, J. W. (1974), *The Farside of Madness*. Englewood Cliffs: Prentice Hall.

Piaget, J. (1962), *Play, Dreams, and Imitation in Childhood*. C. Gattegno and F. M. Hodgson (trans.). New York: Norton.

Piaget, J. (1965), *The Moral Judgment of the Child*. New York: Free Press.

Piaget, J. (1975), *The Child and Reality. Problems of Genetic Psychology*. A Rosin (trans.). New York: Grossman.

Progoff, I. (1969), *Jung's Psychology and its Social Meaning* (2nd edn). New York: Julian Press.

Progoff, I. (1977), *At a Journal Workshop*. New York: Dialogue House.

Read, H. (1963), *The Forms of Things Unknown*. New York: World Publishing Co.

Riegel, K. (1978), *Psychology Mon Amour. A Countertext.* Boston: Houghton Mifflin.

Sanford, N. (1966), *Self and Society.* New York: Atherton.

Sanford, N. (1981), 'Notes toward a theory of personality development at eighty or any old age.' In J.-R. Staude (ed.), *Wisdom and Age.* Berkeley: Ross Books.

Schorske, C. E. (1980), *Fin-de-Siecle Vienna. Politics and Culture.* New York: Alfred A. Knopf.

Sheehy, G. (1976), *Passages. Predictable Crises of Adult Life.* New York: Dutton.

Singer, J. (1973), *Boundaries of the Soul. The Practice of Jung's Psychology.* London: Gollancz.

Staude, J.-R. (1968), *Max Scheler, 1874-1928. An Intellectual Portrait.* New York: The Free Press.

Staude, J.-R. (1976), 'From Depth Psychology to Depth Sociology: Freud, Jung, and Lévi-Strauss,' *Theory and Society*, 3, pp. 303-38.

Staude, J.-R. (1977), *Consciousness and Creativity.* Berkeley: Ross Books.

Staude, J.-R. (1981), *Wisdom and Age.* Berkeley: Ross Books.

Stern, P. J. (1976), *C. G. Jung: The Haunted Prophet.* New York: George Braziller.

Storr, A. (1974), *Jung.* London: Fontana.

Trüb, H. (1962), *Heilung aus der Begegnung. Eine Auseinandersetzung mit der Psychologie C. G. Jungs* (2nd ed). Stuttgart.

Vaillant, G. E. (1977), *Adaptation to Life.* Boston: Little Brown.

Van der Post, L. (1975), *Jung and the Story of our Time.* New York: Pantheon Books.

Von Franz, M. L. (1975), *C. G. Jung. His Myth in our Time.* W. H. Kennedy (trans.). London: Hodder & Stoughton.

Wilson, C. (1972), *New Pathways in Psychology. Maslow and the Post-Freudian Revolution.* London: Gollancz.

Name index

Apollo, 73
Arieti, S., 109
Aristotle, 72
Augustine, 37

Bachofen, J. J., 37
Binswanger, Ludwig, 30-1
Bleuler, Eugene, 29, 34, 43
Boehme, Jacob, 27, 41
Brome, Vincent, 47, 51
Buber, Martin, 106
Bugental, James, F. T., 99
Bühler, Charlotte, 2, 4, 108
Burckhardt, Jacob, 37

Christ, 75, 78

Dante, 68
Darwin, 41
Dubois-Reymond, Emile, 41
Duprel, Karl, 27

Eckhart, Meister, 41
Einstein, Albert, 41
Elijah, 56
Ellenberger, Henri, 32
Erikson, Erik Homberg, 2, 7-9, 108, 109, 111
Eschenmayer, 27

Fitzgerald, F. Scott, 68
Fordham, Michael, 103
Frankl, Victor, 5, 99
Freud, Sigmund, 7, 25, 31-43, 48, 66, 74, 75, 76, 87, 94, 114
Fromm, Erich, 99

God, 89
Goethe, 25-8, 65, 116, 117
Goldstein, Kurt, 17
Gorres, 27
Gross, Otto, 108

Hall, G. Stanley, 3
Hannah, Barbara, 116
Havinghurst, Robert, 2, 3, 5-6, 108
Hegel, G. W. F., 88, 89
Heraclitus, 78
Hesse, Hermann, 68
Hillman, James, 44, 76, 91, 104
Homer, 50
Horney, Karen, 4

Jacoby, Jolande, 116
Jacques, Elliot, 67
Jaffe, Aniela, 116
Janet, Pierre, 31
Jones, Ernest, 33
Jung, Carl Gustav, Sr, 29, 116
Jung, Carl Gustav: *Aion*, 100; 'Analytical psychology and education', 70; childhood, 51; 'The development of personality', 70; development of his theory of individuation, 69-95; 'Diagnostic association studies' (1973), 33; dreams, 64; 'Marriage as a psychological relationship', 70, 97; mid-life crisis, 44-68; *Psychological Types*, 70, 77, 78, 82, 98, 110; *Psychology of Dementia Praecox*, 32; 'The psychology and pathology of so-called occult phenomena' (1970), 27-9; 'The

Subject index